PRIMITIVE BUDDHISM

PRIMITIVE BUDDHISM

ITS ORIGIN AND TEACHINGS

ELIZABETH A. REED, A. M.

GYAN

Published by

GYAN

Gyan Publishing House
5, Ansari Road
Daryaganj, New Delhi-110002
Phone: 011-47034999, 9811692060
E-mail: books@gyanbooks.com

Distribution Network
gyanbooks.com
India, USA, Canada, UK, Australia, France

ISBN: 978-81-212-8622-0 (PB)
First Published, 1896

2nd Impression 2023

Printed at: Gyan Press, Delhi.

PRIMITIVE BUDDHISM
Author: ELIZABETH A. REED

PRIMITIVE BUDDHISM

ITS ORIGIN AND TEACHINGS

BY

ELIZABETH A. REED, A. M.

Member of the Philosophical Society of Great Britain, Member of the International Congress of Orientalists, Author of "Hindu Literature," "Persian Literature," etc.

CHICAGO

SCOTT, FORESMAN & CO.

1896

PRIMITIVE BUDDHISM:

Its Origin and Teachings.

TABLE OF CONTENTS.

CHAPTER I.

PRIMITIVE BUDDHISM.

A BLESSING TO INDIA — A BENEFIT TO WOMAN — CRITICAL STUDY OF BUDDHISM — NUMBER OF ADHERENTS 13

CHAPTER II.

NUMEROUS BUDDHAS.

TWENTY-FOUR PREDECESSORS OF GAUTAMA — DĪPANKARA — KOṆḌAÑÑA — MANGALA— SUMANA—REVATA— SOBHITA — THREE BUDDHAS — PADMUTTARA — SUMEDHA — SUJĀTA — VIPASSIN — SPHERE OF MANIFESTATIONS —HIGHEST ACHIEVEMENT . . . 31

CHAPTER III.

BUDDHISTIC ACCOUNT OF GAUTAMA BUDDHA.

THE LALITA VISTARA—THE JĀTAKA—BIRTH OF GAUTAMA—PHYSICAL SIGNS OF A BUDDHA—HIS MANHOOD—THE FOUR VISIONS—GREAT RENUNCIATION—THE ESCAPE—GREAT TEMPTATION—ATTAINMENT OF BUDDHAHOOD—FIRST CONVERTS—RETURN HOME—FIRST MONASTERY . . . 42

CHAPTER IV.

HISTORIC SKETCH OF BUDDHA.

THE THEORY OF A MYTH—BIRTH AND EARLY LIFE—ASCETICISM—ENLIGHTENMENT—DISCOURSE AT BENARES—SERMON ON THE NON-EXISTENCE OF THE SOUL—THE FIRE SERMON—RELIEF FROM TRANSMIGRATION—THE FATAL MEAL—THE DEATH OF BUDDHA 63

CHAPTER V.

TEACHINGS OF BUDDHISM.

TRANSMIGRATION—FORMER BIRTHS OF BUDDHA—THE JĀTAKAS—THE ORTHODOX BELIEF—VARIOUS FORMS ASSUMED—THE MONKEYS AND THE DEMON—THE WILY ANTELOPE—THE BULL WHO WON THE BET—THE FISH AND HIS WIFE—THE WISE JUDGE . . 82

CHAPTER VI.

THE TEACHINGS OF BUDDHISM, CONCLUDED.

METAPHYSICS — THE SOUL — ATHEISM — POLYTHEISM — IDOLATRY — PRAYER — PESSIMISM — HEAVEN — HELL — SALVATION — MORALITY — NIRVĀṆA — PARI-NIRVĀṆA . . . 104

CHAPTER VII.

THE BUDDHIST ORDER OF MONKS.

ORDINATION OF THE BHIKKHUS, OR MONKS — RULES FOR THEIR DIRECTION — UNSANITARY LAWS — UNSANITARY CLOTHING — PROTECTION FROM VENOMOUS SERPENTS — THE SERPENT WHO JOINED THE ORDER — NUNS — BUDDHA'S PROPHECY — RESULTS OF MONKHOOD 133

CHAPTER VIII.

EARLY BUDDHIST LITERATURE.

LITERARY ACTIVITY IN THE EAST — THE ART OF WRITING — EXTENT OF THE BUDDHIST SCRIPTURES — THE DATE OF THE CANON — THE TRI-PIṬAKA — THE VINAYA TEXTS — CARE OF THE BOWLS — TOOTH STICKS — THE WONDERS OF BUDDHA — GREAT EFFICACY OF RECITATION — INTEGRITY OF THE TEXT 150

CHAPTER IX.

EARLY BUDDHIST LITERATURE, CONTINUED.

THE SECOND PIṬAKA — THE MAHĀ-PARINIBBĀNA — THE PROXIMATE CAUSES OF EARTHQUAKES—THE DHAMMA-PADA—PUNISHMENT —THE SUTTA-NIPĀTA—THE THIRD PIṬAKA—THE MAHĀ-YĀNA, OR NORTHERN SCHOOL —THE BUDDHA-ḲARITA-KĀVYA—THE SŪTRAS OF JAPAN—THE AMITĀYUR-DHYĀNA — THE VAGRAḲ-ḲḤEDIKĀ—THE DOCTRINAL TEACHING OF THE SŪTRA— THE PRAGÑĀ-PĀRAMITĀ — THE TĀNTRA LITERATURE — STRIKING CONTRASTS 163

CHAPTER X.

EARLY BUDDHIST LITERATURE, CONCLUDED.

BUDDHA'S INDEBTEDNESS TO BRĀHMANISM — THE DHAMMA-PADA — SIMILARITIES TO OLD TESTAMENT TEACHINGS — POSSIBLE SOURCES OF INFORMATION — SUMMARY . 183

CHAPTER XI.

CONCLUSION.

PRIMITIVE BUDDHISM IN INDIA—ORIGIN OF THE SYSTEM — ATHEISM — TRANSMIGRATION — KARMA—PESSIMISM—METAPHYSICS — THE ACCUMULATION OF MERIT — NIRVĀṆA—LITERATURE — THE ORIGINALITY OF BUDDHA — CAUSES OF EXTENSIVE INFLUENCE . 198

PREFACE.

THE philosophies of the East have often been presented to the western world during the last few years, and much interest has been awakened, especially in the subject of Buddhism. Although the number of its adherents has been greatly overestimated, still this system controls, to a greater or less extent, the thought of millions of our fellow-beings, and it is entitled to a fair and impartial examination. There are comparatively few people, however, in this busy age, who have time to make an exhaustive research on the subject, and it is thought, therefore, that a comprehensive handbook, which has been carefully prepared, will be welcome to many, who will be glad to learn, quickly and easily, what this philosophy really is.

It is not the object of the present work to follow the system in the various changes through which it has passed, or to discuss the protean forms which it has assumed in modern times, but to present, in as brief a manner as is consistent with accuracy, the authoritative teachings of primitive and genuine Buddhism.

It would appear that such works are greatly needed from the fact that theories have been advocated as the doctrines of Buddhism of which its founder never heard, and statements have been made upon the modern platform which could astonish no one so much as Gautama and his early followers. When speculation is rife upon any subject, the truth can only be obtained by an appeal "to the law and the testimony." Every system has a right to demand that it be judged by its own official documents, and, therefore, the utmost care has been taken to present, in condensed form, the doctrines of the early Buddhists, as set forth in their own standard works.

Quotations have not only been accurately made, but the references are given, so that they may be easily verified, as the books belonging to the Buddhistic canon are now available to the English-speaking world, and they may be found in many of our libraries. Among the best in this respect is the Chicago Public Library, where a wealth of Oriental lore is ever at the service of the student.

The selections in the present volume have been made from the official documents of the early Buddhists, as found in the Sacred Books of the East and elsewhere. These are authorities which no scholar will question, and it will be found that the integrity of the text has been sufficiently maintained.

Besides the books belonging to the canon, the author is indebted to the works and, in some cases, to the private correspondence, also, of the most accomplished Orientalists in the world of scholars. It is a pleasure to acknowledge one's indebtedness to such men as Prof. James Legge, Sir Monier Monier-Williams, K. C. I. E., Prof. F. Max Müller, Rhys Davids, Oldenberg, Prof. A. H. Sayce, Burnouf, Barthélemy Saint Hilaire and others, the credits being given where the quotations are made.

Especial thanks are also due to the distinguished savants who have carefully examined portions of the manuscript, and given it the benefit of their invaluable criticism. The principal points in the tenth chapter were presented by the author, in a paper recently read before the Victoria Institute, or Philosophical Society of Great Britain, and before it was accepted there, it was submitted, by the officers of the Institute, to the leading scholars of the world in this particular field of letters.

Hence, it is offered to the public only after it has been honored, by critical examination and thoughtful discussion, by eminent Orientalists.

Cordial thanks are due the American press for generous notices of the author's previous works, in many instances columns having been devoted to able and discriminating reviews. It is a pleasure, also, to acknowledge the courtesies of the European press, as shown in some of their most influential journals, and the cordial encouragement of distinguished Oriental scholars, whose congratulations and words of approval have been especially grateful.

Technical terms and proper names have been avoided as far as possible, but a few are necessarily used, and diacritical points are given as a guide to the pronunciation.

The work has been prepared in the hope that it may be of real service to careful students in this field of thought, and it is commended to their attention by

THE AUTHOR.

PRONUNCIATION.

A LITTLE attention to the diacritical points will enable the reader to pronounce correctly the musical names of the Buddhists and Hindūs.

In the present volume Sir Monier Monier-Williams' method of transliteration, as presented in his Sanskṛit Grammar, has been chiefly used. The nasal *m*, however, is indicated here, as in the works of Prof. F. Max Müller, by the italic letter.

Diacritical points are omitted from the foot notes, the system of pronunciation being sufficiently indicated in the body of the work.

A—a is pronounced as in rur*a*l.
Ā—ā " " t*a*r, f*a*ther, etc.
I—i " " f*i*ll.
Ī—ī " " pol*i*ce.
U—u " " f*u*ll.
Ṛi—ṛi " " mer*ri*ly.
Ṛī—ṛī " " ma*ri*ne
E—e " " pr*e*y.
Ai—ai " " *ai*sle.
Au—au " " H*au*s (German).
N̲—n̲ sounded like *n* in the French mo*n*.
Ṇ—ṇ " as in *n*o*n*e (nun).

Ṅ—ṅ like *ng* in si*ng* (siṅ).

Ñ—ñ like *n* in si*n*ge.

m (italic) has a nasal sound.

h is a visarga, or a distinctly audible sound aspirate.

K—k sounded like *ch* in *ch*ur*ch*.

Kh—kh	pronounced	as in	in*kh*orn.
G—g	"	"	*g*un.
Gh—gh	"	"	lo*g* *h*ut.
Ć—ć	"	"	dol*c*e (in music), English *ch* as in *ch*urch.
Ṭ—ṭ	"	"	*t*rue.
Ṭh—ṭh	"	"	an*th*ill.
Ḍ—ḍ	"	"	*d*rum.
Ḍh—ḍh	"	"	re*d* *h*aired.
Th—th	"	"	nu*th*ook, though more dental.
Ś—ś	"	"	*s*ure, se*s*sions.
S—s	"	"	*s*ir or mi*ss*.

U in Buddha is pronounced like *oo* in f*oo*d.

PRIMITIVE BUDDHISM

Its Origin and Teachings.

CHAPTER I.

PRIMITIVE BUDDHISM.

A BLESSING TO INDIA—A BENEFIT TO WOMAN—CRITICAL STUDY OF BUDDHISM—NUMBER OF ADHERENTS.

ABOUT the fifth century before our era, there was formulated in India a system of philosophy known as Buddhism. It was the patron of good works, and opposed the priestly tyranny of the Brāhmans. It taught self-denial without self-torture, and inculcated charity, tolerance and humanity. It forbade avarice and discouraged the accumulation of wealth, while it promoted, to a certain extent, both physical and moral progress.

In its primitive form, it was merely a system of philosophy founded upon a pessimistic view of life, but it soon acquired the character of a religion. Still, it made no war upon existing faiths; its advocates claimed that a man could consistently be a Brāhman, a Taoist, or anything else, and at the same time a Buddhist—therefore it made wonderful progress in the East.

Although largely evolved from Brāhmanism, it almost entirely supplanted the older faith upon its native soil, and eventually included in its conquests nearly the whole of Eastern Asia. It was introduced into China in the first century of our era, and soon became one of the three state religions of the empire, although it did not find a home in Japan until hundreds of years later.

It was the ruling intellectual power in India from the time it supplanted Brāhmanism until the fourth or fifth century, when it began to lose its position, although it maintained itself, to a greater or less extent, until the twelfth or thirteenth century. At this time it had become so largely absorbed in the worship of Vishṇu and Śiva that it lost its individuality, and was soon merged into the composite forms of Hindūism.

Surely a system which has for centuries held an important position in history, and which still controls the thought of millions of our race, is entitled to a fair and impartial consideration. An examination, however, of the multitudinous forms of modern Buddhism would occupy several volumes, for it has assumed different phases in every country which it has approached, always assimilating the leading thought of the people whom it sought to proselyte:

It is the province, therefore, of the present work to investigate the system in its primitive and purest form, endeavoring to ascertain what theories and principles were taught by Gautama Buddha and his early followers, and alluding to modern developments only so far as they appear to be the result of such teaching.

In Japan, finding itself unable to displace the earlier systems, it embraced Shintoism, while in Ceylon, Burmah and Siam, it was grafted upon serpent worship, Nāga[1] worship and demon worship, with all of which, as well as the adoration of certain Hindū gods, it is still connected.

In Tibet it was amalgamated with Shamanism,[2] and although combined with magic, and offerings to Śiva, it has an organization similar to the Church of Rome, the Grand Lama being the Pope. They have the celibacy of the priesthood, the worship of the saints, confessions, fasting, processions and holy water. They have, too, the cross and miter, the service with double choirs, the exorcisms, and the censer for incense. It is probable that some of these ideas were derived from Catholicism in later times, but it is true that the practice of celibacy, confession, and fasting existed in Buddhism before the birth of the Roman Church.

Primitive Buddhism was at first opposed to ecclesiastical organization, having no God, no priests and no church. It was simply a brotherhood, consisting of men who had renounced all family ties, and even

[1] The Nagas properly belong to a class of serpent demons, having human faces, with serpent-like lower extremities, and they live in one of the lower regions of the earth.

[2] The principal elements in Shamanism are the worship of nature and the dread of spirits. It has much in common with the lowest types of Saivism, Saktism and Tantrism.—*Williams*.

all desire for life, men who had pledged themselves to devote their time to the recitation of the law, self-restraint and the accumulation of merit, for the sake of their own deliverance. Being opposed to all sacerdotalism and ceremonial observances, it abolished, as far as possible, the sacrificial system of the Brāhmans, and rejected the terrible methods of self-torture, maintaining that a life of purity and morality was better than all the forms and ceremonies of the Vedic ritual.

The first idea implied by Buddhism is intellectual enlightenment, but this must be acquired by man through his own inner consciousness, unaided by external influences. It advocated self-conquest, self-concentration and separation from the world for the attainment of true knowledge, and yet it encouraged association, by establishing a brotherhood of celibate monks. It taught the doctrines of republicanism by admitting to this brotherhood every caste and rank, the humblest Śūdra being as welcome there as the most aristocratic Brāhman. The rich and the poor, the learned and the ignorant, were all bound together by the desire of self-conquest and the common wish to be guided by the doctrines which were promulgated by Buddha.

The new sect remained for a long time obscure, but its success was greatly hastened and, perhaps, largely accomplished by political events. Chandragupta, who was a low-born Śūdra, usurped the throne of Magada, after killing king Nanda. He founded the Maurya dynasty, and extended the kingdom of Magada all over Hindūstān, soon becoming so powerful that the successor of Alexander thought it politic to form an alliance with the Hindū king, and sent an ambassador to reside at his court.

After the death of the king's son, Aśoka, who was the grandson of Chandra-gupta, succeeded to the throne,[1] and became one of the most powerful monarchs of India. This dynasty held its position in defiance of the Brāhmanic priesthood, the kings themselves having been born of the lowest caste; it was, therefore, natural that Aśoka should ally himself with a system which proclaimed equality between the Śūdra and the Brāhman, so far as the brotherhood was concerned, and he made Buddhism the state religion of India.

But there had been serious dissensions in the ranks, even during the time of Buddha, and before long, eighteen schismatic schools of thought were established. Two councils had been held, in order, if possible, to bring order out of chaos, but the resulting controversies were of the most discouraging character, and another became necessary. The third council was, therefore, held at Patna during the sixteenth or seventeenth year of Aśoka's reign.

The whole canon is supposed to have been transmitted orally from one generation to another, even at this time, as the Buddhists do not claim that it was committed to writing earlier than the first century before Christ.[2]

After the third council, missionaries were supported by king Aśoka, and sent in all directions, one of the

[1] About 260 B. C. [2] About 85 B. C.

first being the king's own son, who carried the doctrine into Ceylon. Afterward the system spread over the whole of India and some adjoining countries, while it eventually became the ruling creed of Eastern Asia.

BUDDHISM A BLESSING TO INDIA.

At the time of the rise of the new philosophy, India was burdened to the utmost with a system of caste which recognized neither justice nor mercy. Under this iron law the people were divided into four classes, the first or highest being the Brāhmans, or the priesthood, of whom it was declared that they were "twice born," and even the kings were subject to them. The second was the Kshatriya, or military caste, which included also the kings and the royal families. The third was the Vaiśya, which was composed of the agricultural class, and the fourth was made up of the Śūdras or slaves.

The Brāhmans were numerous and powerful, and they instituted a complicated ceremonial which embraced every public and private act. No marriage could be solemnized without them; no dead could be disposed of, no sick could be properly attended, no household set up, without their ministrations. Every prayer must be prescribed, and every sacrifice determined, for only the Brāhmans knew which deity should be invoked at each particular time, or what offering would please him. Any mistake in reference to the clarified butter, or the length of the ladle used, brought down upon the head of the offender not only the wrath of the priest, but also the fury of the gods. It was impossible to avoid evil without the intervention of the priests, for no one else knew what food could be safely eaten, or what dress might be properly worn, and their services must be amply rewarded. Indeed, Brāhmanism was a system of organized robbery, and the priests made life intolerable for any one who happened to offend them by the smallest seeming neglect.

Not only did this complicated ceremonial embrace every moment of a man's life from the cradle to the grave, but it encouraged the most painful austerities. "Some devotees seated themselves in one spot, and kept perpetual silence, with their legs bent under them, for years. Some ate only at intervals of four, six or fourteen days. Some slept on ashes, gravel, stones, thorny grass or spikes, with the face downward. Some gazed at the sun until totally blind, or sat surrounded by five fires, or rested on one foot, or kept one arm perpetually uplifted, or baked themselves on hot stones, or submerged their bodies in water, or suspended themselves in air."[1]

The object of these self-tortures was a union with the Supreme Being, and this could only be attained by bodily mortification and abstract meditation. As Buddha did not believe in a Supreme Being, he could not advocate these barbarous methods of approaching him. In later times, however, the development of Buddhistic ideas resulted in a connection with this very system, and many Buddhists now hold, with the

[1] Sir Monier Monier-Williams, "Buddhism," p. 228.

Yoga of the Brāhmans, that adepts skilled in occult science may, by a determined effort of will, force out the ethereal body through the pores of the skin, and make this phantasmal form visible in distant places.

Primitive Buddhism taught self-restraint, and preached purity in thought, word and action; it encouraged literature and art, it advocated the principles of fraternity. It elevated the morality of the people by teaching respect for the lives of others, even though its *summum bonum* was the extinction of all life. It was a blessing to India, because it opposed the penitential austerities and self-inflicted sufferings which obtained under the influence of the Brāhmans, and instead of the severe penances and excommunications which were inflicted by the priests for trifling offenses, Buddha at first required only public confession and a promise to abstain from wrong-doing in the future.

It was an advance toward social liberty, as it advocated the republican doctrine of equality in the Brotherhood,[1] and proclaimed that "the highest path" was open to the members of all castes.

It was a blessing to India, in that it opposed the ecclesiastical tyranny of a well paid priesthood, but it must be confessed that the charitable gifts which had been monopolized by the Brāhmans did not contribute to the comfort of the oppressed people; they merely

[1] Although the secret of Buddha's success lay in his disregard of the privileges of the priestly class, still he did not wish to abolish caste as a social institution, and there is no trace of social or democratic communism in any of his sermons. His only attacks were leveled against the exclusive privileges claimed by the Brahmans, and against their cruel treatment of the lower castes.—*Max Müller, Chips, Vol. II, p. 337.*

began to flow into new channels, supporting hundreds of thousands of Buddhist mendicants. And even to-day, births and marriages, illness and death, are great sources of revenue to the Buddhistic priesthood.

It was a blessing, in so far as it advocated the principles of kindness, and it did good service for the time in promoting literature and art, and inculcating the doctrine of the accumulation of merit by good actions. It was a great improvement upon Brāhmanism, even though its final hope was the abolition of suffering by the abolition of existence.

A BENEFIT TO WOMAN.

Although Buddhism made war upon the home by enjoining monkhood,—it commanded men who were already married to abandon their wives and children, to lay aside all efforts to make a livelihood in a legitimate way, and take up their abode with the monks who begged their bread from door to door—although it declared that "the life of woman is always darkness,"[1] still it was a benefit to woman, in that it allowed her to become a nun, under the same rules which obtained in communities of men, and thus attain to a semblance of equality. The system also admitted "lay brothers and lay sisters," married householders and working men, for Buddha saw that this course was necessary. If all Buddhists were monks and nuns, there would be no work done, and no food produced, hence the communities must be depopulated by starvation. Nevertheless these

[1] Buddha-karita, I, 17. This work is assigned to the first century.

married householders could not attain to "the highest path."

Buddhists do not require the imprisonment of wives and daughters in the Zenānás, as do the Mohammedans and Brāhmans; on the contrary the women of the family are sometimes introduced to European guests, and allowed to converse freely. The child marriages, which constitute one of the most terrible curses of India, are not enforced in Buddhist countries, for there the bridegroom is seldom less than eighteen years of age.

"Women," says Renan, "were indebted to Buddhism for a momentary amelioration of their fate. The new religion gave them religious importance. They were permitted to embrace monastic life, and to practice the same rule as men. No doubt they preserved a notable inferiority; they could not directly arrive at the state of Buddha, but they were enabled to reach that state by being born again as men. The female sex continued to be a punishment. In the state of perfection there will be no women.

"The miracle of a change of sex is quite frequent in the Buddhist legends. The accomplished woman becomes a man. That is what happened to Sugāta's daughter, who achieved perfection. Transformed into a man, she seated herself beneath the tree of intelligence and entered into supreme rest."[1]

Great respect has always been paid by Buddhists to the various forms of animal life; so strong was this sentiment that people could "accumulate merit" by purchasing birds (which professional bird catchers

[1] Renan, "Studies in Religious History," p. 107.

entrapped for that purpose), and giving them liberty. All animals are more or less venerated, for, according to the theory of transmigration, they are liable to be the different forms of one's ancestors; and not only this, but the Buddha is supposed to have been incarnated in many of them. It may be for this reason that the serpent, the bull, the pig, the monkey, and many others, are regarded as peculiarly sacred.

But with all this veneration for animal life, it must be confessed that during the long centuries of the supremacy of Buddhism in India, infants were sometimes sacrificed and living women were burned upon the dead bodies of their husbands. For two thousand years the horrible custom of the suttee prevailed in India, until it was abolished by the British government in 1830, and it is difficult to understand why Buddhism, with all its reverential care for animal, serpent and insect life, did not extend its protection to women and children. It is true that Buddhism did not prevent the sacrifice of her children, or save her from being burned alive, but it accorded to woman a certain amount of social freedom, and also permitted her to become a nun, although she was even then constantly under the dominion of the monks.

CRITICAL STUDY OF BUDDHISM.

Although this system has been a real power in the world for centuries, and still dominates the thought of millions of the human race, it was comparatively unknown in the western world until very modern times.

India was scarcely more than a name to the scholars of the eighteenth century, and what information they had on the subject was derived, more or less at random, from China, Tartary, Japan, Tibet, and other countries, where it had been transplanted from its native soil.

During the last fifty years, however, scholars have made marvelous progress in the way of collecting, classifying and translating the literature belonging to this department of Oriental lore. The scientific study of the subject really began soon after the discovery of the original documents by Mr Hodgson, who was then living in Nepāl as the political resident of the East India Company. This distinguished worker in Oriental fields succeeded in sending about sixty volumes of these works to the Asiatic Society of Bengal, and after a time he sent two complete collections of the same manuscripts to the Asiatic Society of London and the Société Asiatique of Paris.

While Mr. Hodgson's discoveries were attracting the attention of scholars in Calcutta, a Hungarian scholar named Alexander Csoma de Körös traveled on foot from Hungary to Tibet, and learned the language, which no European, up to his time, had ever mastered. He then explored the great collection of the canonical books of the Buddhists preserved in that language, but without the cordial co-operation of the members of the Asiatic Society he could have accomplished little, as the canon of the Tibetans, containing many repetitions, exceeds in bulk the sacred books of any other nation.

Almost contemporaneously with these discoveries, a Russian by the name of Schmidt centered his efforts upon the Mongolian language, and after a time he was able to translate portions of the Mongolian version of the canon. Within a very few years George Turnour presented to the world of scholars the Buddhist literature of Ceylon, written in the ancient Pāli characters.[1] And thus, within the space of ten years, the science of letters was enriched by the accession of four complete Buddhist literatures.

The manuscripts belonging to the Société Asiatique in Paris fell into the hands of Burnouf, and after seven years of labor that distinguished savant published his "Introduction á l'Histoire du Buddhism,"[2] and this book seems to have laid the foundation of the systematic study of the subject. Other enthusiastic scholars took up the work, so that in these later years we need be no longer ignorant of the historic facts concerning Buddhism, either in its primitive form or its later developments.

Translations of the text of the Pāli canon have been made by Childers, Oldenberg, Rhys Davids, Morris, Fausböll and others. The world is also largely indebted for information on this subject to the works of Lassen, Turnour, Hardy, Gogerly, Williams, Weber, Bigandet, Max Müller, Kern, Cowell, Senart and others.

It is a theme which furnishes abundant material for those who choose to follow it in all its numerous changes, for Buddhism has developed into contradictory

[1] Some scholars suppose that the Pali resulted from an artificial infusion of Sanskrit. It is claimed that nearly two-fifths of the Pali vocabulary consists of unmodified Sanskrit. It probably represented the prevailing dialect of the time, and is sometimes called Tanti.

[2] Published in 1844.

systems in different countries, presenting a new phase in each locality, while in India, the land of its birth, it changed greatly even during the first ten years of its existence.

M. Barthélemy Saint-Hilaire, who has been called "the first historian of Buddhism," in his critical work on this subject, says: "It is the misfortune of our times that the doctrines which form the foundation of Buddhism meet, at the hands of some of our philosophers, with a favor which they ill deserve. For some years we have seen systems arising in which metempsychosis and transmigration are highly spoken of, and attempts are made to explain the world and man, without either a God or a Providence, exactly as Buddha did. A future life is refused to the yearnings of mankind. God is dethroned, and in his place they substitute man, the only being, we are told, in which the infinite becomes conscious of itself. These theories are recommended to us, sometimes in the name of science, or of history, or of philology, and even metaphysics; and although they are neither new nor very original, yet they can do much injury to feeble hearts.

"This is not the place to examine such theories, and the authors are too sincere to be condemned without discussion, but they should know, by the example of Buddhism, what becomes of man if he depends upon himself alone, and if his meditations, misled by a pride of which he is hardly conscious, bring him to the precipice where Buddha was lost."[1]

[1] "Le Bouddha et sa Religion," Par Barthélemy Saint-Hilaire, Membre de l'Institut. Int. p. vii.

If such be the opinions, not only of one of the most distinguished scholars of France, but of many savants who have devoted years of their lives to the scientific investigation of the subject, many will wonder that the system has attracted so much attention in the world of letters. But truth is never satisfied without the fullest and most critical investigation, and hence men like Burnouf did not shrink from the task of acquiring a practical knowledge of Tibetan, Pāli, Singhalese and Burmese, as well as Sanskṛit, in order to qualify themselves for the work of doing full justice to the subject.

The translation of a Buddhistic work from Chinese into French would seem comparatively easy for a scholar who understood both languages, but M. Stanislaus Julien, who has long been considered one of the most accomplished Chinese scholars of Europe, was obliged to spend twenty years of hard work in order to prepare himself for the task.

Such are the intricacies of the subject, as connected with the various languages through which it has passed, that he was compelled to acquire a working knowledge of Sanskṛit, and study the Buddhist literatures, not only in that language, but also in Pāli, Tibetan, Mongolian and Chinese.

It is such pioneer work as this which prepares the way for the great host of scholars in any department of science or letters; much labor is performed by the few for the benefit of many, but the results are invaluable. "Many are the advantages," says F. Max Müller, "to be derived from a careful study of other religions, but the greatest of all is, that it teaches us to appreciate more truly what we have in our own. . . . Let us see what other nations have had, and still have, in the place of religion — let us examine the prayers, the worship, the theology, even of the most highly civilized races — the Greeks, the Romans, the Hindūs, the Persians — and we shall then understand more thoroughly what blessings are vouchsafed to us in being allowed to breathe, from the first breath of life, the pure air of Christian life and knowledge. We are too apt to take the greatest blessings as a matter of course, and even religion forms no exception. We have done so little to gain our religion, we have suffered so little in the cause of truth, that, however highly we prize our own Christianity, we never prize it enough until we have compared it with the religions of the rest of the world."[1]

NUMBER OF ADHERENTS.

It has been customary to claim that "a majority of the human race believe in the doctrines of Buddha," and others, although less sanguine, are still giving currency to the statement that, out of the fifteen hundred millions of the earth's inhabitants, at least five hundred millions are Buddhists.

These incredible figures appear to be obtained by calculating the *entire population of the countries* where the system has a foothold. It should be remembered, however, that Buddhism has disappeared from India proper, although it is still predominant in

[1] Max Müller, Chips, Vol. I, p. 180.

Burmah and Ceylon. Its strongest position is in China and Japan, but in China the principal religion is Confucianism. The best authorities upon this subject, including Dr. James Legge, the professor of Chinese at Oxford University, are of the opinion that there are not more than one hundred millions of real Buddhists in the world.

"I should be surprised," says Professor Legge, "if it were proved that there are one hundred millions of men in this world who would write down, or direct another to enter, their names as believers in Śākyamuni and his doctrines."[1]

Although the question of the truth or falsity of a position can never be indicated by the number of its adherents, still it is necessary to consider the numerical strength of a people in order to ascertain, to some extent, the influence which they exert in the world of thought.

According to the most reliable information which can be obtained concerning the present status of the principal religions of the world, they rank in point of numbers as follows: Christianity, Confucianism, Brāhmanism and Hindūism,[2] Buddhism, Mohammedanism, and lastly Taoism, (the system of Lao-tsze). Jainism, Zoroastrianism and others are too small numerically to be considered in this estimate.[3]

Thus it will be seen that Buddhism occupies numerically the fourth rank, and although its ad-

[1] Trans. Ninth International Congress of Orientals. Vol. II, p. 580.

[2] Brahmanism and Hinduism are practically one system, the latter being merely the expansion of the former.

[3] Williams, B., p. xv.

herents often claim that their creed controls the thought of "the greater portion of the world's population," science must deal with figures and not in fanciful speculations.

It is possible that an exact census might result in some variation of the above estimate, but we must admit that Buddhism is gradually losing its hold on the vast populations which were once loyal to its teachings. It was a blessing to India so far as it opposed Brāhmanism, but China had been, and still is, to a great extent, ruled by the lessons inculcated in her ancient classics, which were formulated by Confucius, and hence Professor Legge says: "Buddhism has been in China but a disturbing influence, ministering to the element of superstition which plays so large a part in the world. I am far from saying the doctrine of the literati is perfect, nevertheless, it has kept the people of China together in national union, passing through many revolutions, but still enduring, after at least four or five millenniums of its existence, and still not without measure of heart and hope. Europe and America can give it something better than India did, in sending it Buddhism in our first century, and I hope they will do so. You must not look to the civilization of China and Japan for the fruits of Buddhism. Go to Tibet and Mongolia, and in the bigotry and apathy of the population, in their prayer wheels and cylinders you will find the achievement of the doctrine of Buddha."[1]

[1] Trans. Ninth International Congress of Orientalists. Vol. II, p. 580.

CHAPTER II.

NUMEROUS BUDDHAS.

TWENTY-FOUR PREDECESSORS OF GAUTAMA — DĪPANKARA — KOṆḌAÑÑA — MANGALA — SUMANA—REVATA — SOBHITA — THREE BUDDHAS — PADMUTTARA — SUMEDHA — SUJĀTA — VIPASSIN — SPHERE OF MANIFESTATIONS— HIGHEST ACHIEVEMENT.

ANY historic outline of early Buddhism must begin with the life of Gautama, but the subject cannot be approached in chronological order without first giving some attention to those who are said to have preceded him, and in whose presence he made his resolve.

We find countless numbers of Buddhas who appear at intervals in a series which has neither beginning nor end. The development of this endless chain, reaching back into the immeasurable past, requires so many kalpas[1] of ages that the eons of geologic time are lost in comparison.

[1] According to some authorities a kalpa is definitely stated as two billion one hundred and sixty millions of years, while others express its duration as follows: "Let it be supposed that a solid rock sixteen miles high, and the same in length and breadth, were lightly rubbed once in a hundred years with a piece of the finest cloth, and by this slight friction reduced to the size of a mango seed—that would give you no idea of the length of a Buddhist kalpa."—*Williams*, B., p 120.

Buddha himself enumerates only eighty-one predecessors, beginning with Dīpankara,[1] but there is a passage in the Larger Sukhāvatī-vyhūa to the effect that there are "many hundred thousands of koṭis[2] of Buddhas, endless like the sand of the Ganges, the incomparable lords."[3]

When we consider that each of these teachers must pass through a long series of births, and can appear only in distinct ages, we cannot wonder that the Buddhist includes a countless number of centuries in his computation of time. Indeed, he does not count the past ages by centuries, but by kalpas and asankheyyas.[4]

The statement that a great number of Buddhas appeared in the past is sometimes offered as an explanation of the numberless changes in Buddhism, and the great number of contradictory systems which are taught. It is claimed that all the conflicting creeds and ceremonies are dim recollections or corruptions of the law which countless Buddhas had preached in countless ages before Gautama, and will continue to preach in ages to come.

TWENTY-FOUR PREDECESSORS OF GAUTAMA.

It is said that even during the ages which elapsed after Gautama had formed a wish to become a Bud-

[1] See the Larger Sukhavati-vyhua, p, ix.

[2] A koti is explained as being ten millions.

[3] Sukhavati-vyhua, 4, 6. See also Lalita Vistara, chap. i, p. 6.

[4] Asankheyya is a word which conveys the idea of innumerable or incalculable. "If for three years it should rain incessantly over the whole surface of the earth, the number of drops falling in such a space of time, although far exceeding human conception, would only equal the number of years in an asankheyya."—*Buchanan, Asiatic Res., VI.*

dha, one hundred and twenty-five thousand enlightened ones appeared, and during this time Gautama was born a multitude of times, and he also met many of his predecessors during his numerous transmigrations. But we have no definite information concerning this multitude until we come to the last twenty-four who preceded him. Concerning these, however, we have many particulars which are given in various standard works. One of the oldest and most highly valued of the Buddhistic classics is a work called "The Jâtakas, or Birth Stories." Indeed, these stories may be safely considered the earliest authority upon this subject, for Rhys Davids says: "The bas reliefs afford indisputable evidence that the 'Birth Stories' were already, *at the end of the third century, B. C.*, considered so sacred that they were chosen as the subjects to be represented around the most sacred Buddhist buildings."[1]

In this work the name of each of the twenty-four is given, and also the names of his parents, the length of his reign, the length of his life, the names of his two principal disciples and of his personal attendants. Even the different trees under which these teachers achieved supreme wisdom are specified. We quote briefly from this authority as follows:

DĪPANKARA.

"The first of the twenty-four Buddhas who preceded Gautama bore the name of Dīpankara (Light Causer). This Buddha was 'he of the mighty jaw

[1] "Buddhist Birth Stories," p. lix.

and broad shoulder,' and who, even at a distance of four thousand leagues, awakened the people to a knowledge of the truth."

"Eighty cubits in height, the great sage Dīpankara shone conspicuous as a noble Sal tree in full bloom. The tree under which he achieved perfection was the banyan, and a hundred thousand years was his age . . . having flamed like a mass of fire, he died, together with his disciples, and all this power, this glory, these jewels on his feet — *all is wholly gone.* Are not all existing things vanity?" During his reign the Bodhisat, who was afterward Gautama Buddha, was a hermit having matted hair.

KOṆḌAÑÑA.

Next to Dīpankara Buddha, after the lapse of one asankheyya, the Teacher Koṇḍañña appeared. He had three assemblies of priests, and the first of these numbered a million of millions. His tree was the Sal, and his life lasted one hundred thousand years.

MANGALA.

The successor of Koṇḍañña was Mangala Buddha, and he also had a million millions of priests in his first assembly, and ten thousand millions at the second. On account of the great merit which he acquired in a former existence, the luster of Mangala Buddha permanently filled ten thousand worlds, just as the luster of the others extended to the distance of a fathom.

It is said that when he was performing the duties of a Bodhisat, or future Buddha, in a former existence, he lived with his wife and children on a mountain. One day a demon, named "sharp fanged," came to him and asked him for his children, and such was the great benevolence of the Bodhisat that he cheerfully and joyously gave them up. The demon, standing at one end of the cloistered walk, devoured the children like a bunch of roots, while the father looked contentedly on. Not a particle of sorrow arose in the Bodhisat as he saw the mouth of the demon covered with blood, but, instead, a great joy welled up within him, as he thought "my gift was well given," and he besought the gods that, in consequence of the great merit of this act, rays of light might one day issue from his body in every direction. It was in consequence of this, that the light emitted from his body filled so large a space.

SUMANA.

After Mangala had lived ninety thousand years and died, the teacher named Sumana appeared. His body was ninety cubits in height, and he also lived ninety thousand years.

During his reign, the Bodhisat, who was afterward born as Gautama, was the Nāga king, mighty and powerful. Hearing that a Buddha had appeared, he left the Nāga world,[1] accompanied by his assembled kinsmen, and made offerings to the Buddha, whose retinue was a million millions of monks, and gave to each of them two garments of fine cloth.

[1] The Naga world was the world of serpent demons. The lower regions are supposed to be peopled with serpents having jewels in their heads. Gautama Buddha was born four times as a serpent.

REVATA.

"After Sumana came the leader named Revata;
The Conqueror unequaled, incomparable, unmatched, supreme."

SOBHITA.

"After Revata came the leader named Sobhita,
Subdued and mild, unequaled, and unrivaled."

THREE BUDDHAS.

"After Sobhita, when an asankheyya had elapsed, three Buddhas were born in one kalpa. The first of these was Anomadassin, and his height was fifty cubits, and his age was one hundred thousand years."

The second of the three was named Paduma, and during his reign, he who was afterward Gautama, having been born a lion,[1] walked around the teacher with reverence and thrice he uttered a mighty roar. For seven days he kept in attendance there, not seeking for prey. Then the teacher looked upon the lion and said: "Hereafter thou shalt become a Buddha."

The third Buddha in this kalpa was named Narada, and the great crimson tree was his Bo-tree. At this time, he who was afterward Gautama, gave a great donation to the Order and made an offering of sandal wood.

After the three Buddhas had been born in one kalpa, the next great teacher was Padmuttara, who was succeeded by Sumedha.

[1] Gautama Buddha was born ten times as a lion.

"Then was born the leader Sujāta, mighty jawed and grandly framed, whose measure none can take."

After him, when eighteen hundred world cycles had passed away, three Buddhas were again born in one kalpa. In the following era there was only one, whose name was Siddhata, and then two Buddhas again appeared in one kalpa.

VIPASSIN.

After these, ninety world cycles ago, there appeared the Blessed One named Vipassin. He, like all the others, had three assemblies of priests, and at the first there were six million and eight hundred thousand monks present. He was eighty cubits in height, and the effulgence of his body always reached a hundred leagues. His age was one hundred thousand years. During the reign of Vipassin, he who was afterward Gautama, having been born as a powerful snake king, gave to the Blessed One a golden chair. He then received the promise that in ninety-one world cycles he should become a Buddha.

After Vipassin came five others, and then the present supreme Buddha.[1]

In the inscription upon the great bell at Ragnun it is stated that with the eight hairs of Gautama enshrined in the dagoba of the temple, there are also "the three divine relics of the three deities who were his immediate predecessors." And in the fourth century of the Christian era there was certainly a sect of Buddhists near to Srāvasti who rejected Gautama,

[1] "Buddhist Birth Stories," Vol. I., pp. 29–55.

reverencing only the three preceding Buddhas, especially one whose body they believed to be buried under one of the dagobas, at which they, as well as the orthodox Buddhists, worshiped.[1]

SPHERE OF MANIFESTATIONS.

Having briefly sketched a few outlines pertaining to the predecessors of Gautama, the sphere of the manifestation of each Buddha follows as a natural sequence. In the Tri-piṭāka, or sacred canon of the Buddhists, there is a treatise which is one of the most popular works in Japan.[2] One of their great scholars asserts that "it is a very able exposition and defense of Buddhism."[3] From this standard work we quote as follows:

"According to the teaching of Buddhism, when a Buddha comes forth to his manifestation three great chiliocosms constitute the sphere of his successful operation. Let us speak of it in one of those worlds. In the midst of every world there is a great Sumēru mountain rising in the great ocean and ascending above nine tiers of the sky. Round the waist of this mountain revolve the sun and moon, separating the day and night. On the four sides of Sumēru are four continents. . . . Above the Sumēru is what we call the Dēva-loka of the four kings. Above this is the Dēva-loka of Shākra. Higher still . . . are

[1] Rhys Davids, B., p. 181.

[2] "A Fair and Dispassionate Discussion of the Three Doctrines Accepted in China," by Liu Mi, a Buddhist writer. Bunyiu Nanjio, in his catalogue of the Tri-pitaka, enters this work as No. 1,643, and adds that the author was of the Yuan dynasty.

[3] Mr. Nanjio in conversation with Professor Legge.

the four Dēva-lokas, having the general name of 'Regions of Desire.' Still higher are the eighteen Dēva-lokas, having the name of 'Regions of Form.' Higher still are the 'Regions Without Form.' All living beings in these regions are subject to birth, old age and death.

Such is the account of one world, and a thousand worlds are called a small chiliocosm, and a thousand such small chiliocosms are called a medium one. A thousand of these are called a great chiliocosm, comprising ten million worlds. The thousand of these being taken three times form only one great chilio-universe. This is the sphere of the successful operation of one Buddha. In this way there are ten thousand million Buddhas, each assigned to his own material region, and they proceed to transform and deliver the ten thousand million worlds till all that are in them, produced from the womb, from eggs or from water, with feet or without feet, with form or without form, with thought or without thought, and even those who have never approximated thought—all are carried across to Nirvāṇa."[1]

THE HIGHEST ACHIEVEMENT OF BUDDHISM.

The same learned author also points out the highest achievement as follows: "Therefore, the learners of Buddhism know the emptiness (and vanity) of all the Skandhas—the constituent elements, that

[1] This extract has necessarily been greatly condensed. See the translation of Dr. James Legge, professor of Chinese in Oxford University.—*Trans. Ninth International Congress of Orientalists, Vol. II., p. 571.*

is, every personality. . . . Amidst their practice of the rules of doctrine they will forget themselves for the sake of other creatures, as when Śākya-muni endured the pain and cut off a piece of his flesh to feed the hawk, or as when he gave his body to feed the famished tigress, and that without fright or apprehension. His money, pearls, treasures — his kingdom, wife, and son — he threw away as he would a worn-out shoe. From life to life, through hundreds, thousands, myriads and lakhs of kalpas, this mind underwent no change. From kalpa to kalpa, through hundreds, thousands and lakhs of kalpas, this mind became more earnest and resolute.

"This is the highest achievement of Buddhism — here it stops. The Sūtra of the Lotus of the law says 'the Tathāgata is the greatest instance of cause and effect.' Therefore, when one comes forth and is manifested in the world, he wishes to cause all living beings to arrive at the same result as himself, for he has sworn that all possessed of an active, intelligent nature shall, with himself, arrive at the unsurpassable consummation of Nirvāṇa."[1]

We have seen, therefore, that the standard authorities of Buddhism are very positive in their declaration that a countless number of Buddhas appeared before Gautama, and the chronicles furnish the names and many other particulars concerning some of them. And not only this, but they furnish a full exposition of the vastness of the system in teaching that "millions of

[1] Legge's Translation.—*Trans. Ninth Congress of Orientalists, Vol. II, pp. 571–574.*

worlds" constitute the sphere of the successful operation of one Buddha." We have seen, also, the highest achievement of Buddhism, which is the absorption, not only of the millions of Buddhas, but also of the millions of worlds and all the life that they contain, into the bosom of "the formless and void"—the Nirvāṇa.

CHAPTER III.

BUDDHISTIC ACCOUNT OF GAUTAMA BUDDHA.

THE LALITA VISTARA — THE JĀTAKA — BIRTH OF GAUTAMA — PHYSICAL SIGNS OF A BUDDHA — HIS MANHOOD — THE FOUR VISIONS — GREAT RENUNCIATION — THE ESCAPE — GREAT TEMPTATION — ATTAINMENT OF BUDDHAHOOD — FIRST CONVERTS — RETURN HOME — FIRST MONASTERY.

GAUTAMA is represented as being the fourth Buddha in the present cycle of time, and there are many difficulties in the way of procuring an account of his life which shall be truly historic.

First, it is a well known fact that, while the people of India are poetic and some of their literature is very beautiful, still they seem to be entirely deficient in what is termed "the historic sense," and hence there is scarcely anything in their annals which can be called history.

Again, it is well understood that nothing was written in relation to Gautama until hundreds of years after his death, the statements concerning his life and teachings having been handed down orally for a long time. "After the Nirvāṇa of Buddha," says the Sarasagraha, "for the space of four hundred and fifty years the text and commentaries, and all the works of

Tathāgata, were preserved and transmitted, by wise priests, orally."[1] If this be true, and Sir M. Monier-Williams is correct concerning the date of Buddha's death,[2] it shows that all the manuscripts on this subject belong to the Christian era.

The Buddhists claim that their first books were written in the latter part of the first century before Christ,[3] but concerning the older portions of the Pāli texts, Professor Oldenberg, the eminent Pāli scholar, says: "They contain neither a biography of Buddha nor the slightest trace of the former existence of any such work."[4]

We have, indeed, the "Book of the Great Decease," which is supposed to belong to an early date, but it treats merely of the incidents connected with his death, or shortly preceding it. And we have, too, the Mahāvagga (although its age is disputed), which contains an account of the first events after Gautama's attainment of Buddhahood, but it is nevertheless true that "any really historical, matter-of-fact life of Buddha, like that of the life of Christ by the four Evangelists, may be looked for in vain in all the Buddhist scriptures. The Buddha's biography is mixed up with such monstrous legends, absurd figments and extravagant fables that to attempt the sifting out of any really historical element, worthy of being compared with the pregnant

[1] Sara-sagraha, quoted by Max Müller. See Science of Rel., note to p. 16.

[2] Williams gives 420 B. C. "as a round number," while Kern makes it still later, giving 388 as the most probable date.

[3] Sa. Bks. E., Vol. X, Int. p. xxv. See also the Mahavansa, p. 287, and the Dipavamsa, Ch. XIX, XX.

[4] Oldenberg, "Buddha, sein Leben, seine Lehre, seine Gemeinde," S. 78.

simplicity, the dignified brevity, of the biography of Christ, would be an idle task."[1]

All the biographies which we have of him are necessarily derived from native sources; we must, therefore, appeal to the earliest Buddhistic documents obtainable, and draw the story of his life from the works which hold the highest position in the opinion of his followers.

THE LALITA VISTARA.

This is one of the most important of the early works, as it is a standard authority with the Northern Buddhists, and is the eighth of the series called the "Nine Dhammas." Concerning the age of this work, however, there is a wide difference of opinion, and so many conjectures have been made that, perhaps, it is only safe to say that it is a poem of unknown authorship and chronology.

The native scholar, Rājendralāla Mitra (who published the work in Sanskṛit, and who has also given us an English version of a portion of it), says in reference to the date of its origin. "We have nothing more positive than inference founded upon insufficient conjecture."[2]

T. W. Rhys Davids remarks that "it is a poem of unknown date and authorship, but probably composed in Nepāl, by some Buddhist poet, who lived between six hundred and a thousand years after the death of Buddha."[3]

1 Williams, B., p. 553.
2 Lalita Vistara. Int. p. 48 (Bibliotheca Indica).
3 "Origin and Growth of Religion" (Hibbert Lectures, 1881), p 197.

M. Foucaux has published a French translation of this work from the Tibetan version, which he claims existed in the sixth century of the Christian era. He also assigns the Sanskṛit original to the Council of King Kanishka,[1] whose reign was during the first century of our era, but Rhys Davids declares that "he does this without any evidence whatever."[2] Sir M. Monier-Williams thinks that it may be as old as the second century of our era.[3]

We shall be compelled to refer to it occasionally, as it is one of the most popular works of the Buddhists, and forms a portion of their sacred canon, but, fortunately, we have an earlier standard authority called

THE JĀTAKA.

The date of this work also is undecided, but Rhys Davids supposes that "the rise of our Jātaka book was due to the religious faith of the Indian Buddhists of the third and fourth century before Christ," the statements therein contained having been handed down orally from time to time until they were committed to writing.

If this be true, we here get very near to the primitive faith of the Buddhists in relation to the subject under consideration.

[1] Kanishka was the third of three brothers, who began to reign in the first century after Christ, and he was a very zealous Buddhist. He called a council of five hundred monks, but unfortunately nothing was done toward settling the canon, as the monks satisfied themselves with the drawing up of three commentaries.

[2] Rhys Davids, B., p. 2. For other opinions on this subject see Senart, p. 496, and Freer, Journal Asiatique, 1886, p. 275, and others.

[3] Williams, B., p. 70.

Although it is briefly called the Jātaka Book, its full title is "The Commentary on the Jātakas," as it not only contains the stories of previous births, but also an explanation of the verses which occur in each story. It contains, too, an introduction to each of them, giving the occasion on which they are said to have been told.

The first part of this commentary contains the life of Gautama down to the time when he revisited his home, after his appearance as a public teacher. "And down to that time," says Rhys Davids, "*it is the best authority we have.*"[1]

The book opens with the following statement: "The Apaṇṇaka and other births which, in times gone by, were recounted on various occasions by the illustrious sage (Gautama) . . . were all collected together, and added to the canon of the scriptures by those who made the recension of the scriptures, and rehearsed them under the name of Jātaka."[2]

This being the best authority we have, we condense the following from the Jātaka, except where credit is given to the Lalita Vistara, the Buddha-karita,[3] or other popular authorities.

THE BIRTH OF GAUTAMA.

"For an infinite number of years the Bodhisat had steadfastly desired to become a Buddha. It was for

[1] Rhys Davids, B., p. 13. This author claims that the original Pali text of this commentary was committed to writing in Ceylon, probably about the middle of the fifth century of our era.

[2] The Nidanakatha, p. 1.

[3] The Buddha-karita is assigned to the first century after Christ.—*Sa. Bks, of the East, Vol. XLIX, Int. p. i.*

this that he persisted in enduring toil, trouble and pain—for this he bore the miseries of life through an unaccountable number of transmigrations, and no suffering ever turned his thoughts from his one great object—the Buddhahood. He cut off portions of his flesh and gave them in alms so many times that, if they were collected, the various portions thus given would make a mass larger than this world. He poured out his blood in alms more than there is water in the great ocean. He gave his head so many times that the heap would be higher than the mightiest of mountains. He gave his eyes more times than there are stars in the skies. He also gave his children to be slaves, and gave his wife away to a Brāhman."[1]

It was in consequence of these great acts of merit that he became a Buddha, and when the proper time arrived he entered the womb of his mother "in the form of an elephant, of a yellowish white color, having six tusks," and the mother also dreamed that she saw him thus enter her body.[2]

When he was born into this world the angels received him in a golden net, and from their hands four kings received him on a cloth of antelope skins, soft to the touch, such as are used on occasions of royal state. . . . Searching in ten directions, and finding no one like himself, he took seven strides, saying, "This is the best direction," and as he walked the Archangel Brahmā held over him the white umbrella, and the Archangel Suyāma followed him with

[1] Pathoma Sompothiyan, p. 89.

[2] The Lalita Vistara, the Buddha-karita and other works give this as an actual fact, some of them relating the dream also, while other authors only relate the story of the dream.

the fan, and other deities with other symbols of royalty in their hands. Then stopping at the seventh step, he sent forth his noble voice, and shouted: "I am the chief of the world."[1]

PHYSICAL SIGNS OF A BUDDHA.

Many authorities tell us that Buddha was born with certain peculiarities of person, which, according to Vedic tradition, indicated that a man would become either a supreme emperor of the world, or a supreme teacher. There are thirty-two of the principal peculiarities and eighty secondary characteristics, which are found in various Buddhistic works of comparatively early date. The tradition of a representation of the wheel (Ćakra), which is said to have existed on the sole of his foot, is confirmed as an ancient idea by the sculptures which formerly adorned the topes, or holy relic mounds of Sanchi and Amravatti in India. The remains of these ancient sculptures furnish ample proof of the faith of the early Buddhists in these peculiar marks.

It is said that even from childhood the body of Buddha was marked with all the signs of eminence. "The soles of his feet are full fleshed and perfectly flat, like golden sandals. They move, not like the feet of an ordinary mortal, but they both touch the ground and leave it at the same time. On each of his feet is a figure of the beautiful Ćakra, with its thousand rays or spokes, and around it are one hun-

[1] The Lalita Vistara puts much more to the same effect into the speech of the newly born babe. See the version of Rajendralala, chap. vii, p. 195. See also Buddha-karita, I. 40,

dred and eight other figures, which appear as a guard of honor around that most excellent sign. The heel of the prince is not like that of other men, but long and projecting. It is smooth and round as a ball of thread, and excels in beauty the heel of any other being. This extraordinary length of heel is one of the signs of a Grand Being, the length of his fingers and toes is another. His feet are not jointed to the ankle in the usual manner, but the ankle rises from the center of the foot, and is so formed that, without the trouble of moving his feet, he can turn his whole body in any direction he pleases. His knees are round, full and fleshy, with the bone in the center. His arms are so long that he can, without stooping, touch his knees with his hands. His skin is perfect; his glossy black hairs grow one by one, curling upward. Between his shoulders there is no depression; his arms are round and smooth. His back has no depression in the center, but is flat as a golden plank. He has about seven thousand nerves of taste converging at the throat, by means of which he has the sensation of taste all over the body. His jaw is like that of a lion; he has forty teeth, even and perfect as a row of gems. He has four canine teeth, or tusks, white, and gleaming like planets. His tongue is soft and flexible, and long enough to reach his forehead. On his forehead, between his eyebrows, is a spiral tuft of long white hairs turning to the right. These are the signs of the Grand Being."[1]

[1] Pathoma Sompothiya, pp. 110, 115. Lalita Vistara, chap. vii, p. 42 (Rajendralala Mitra's Trans.) Also Buddha-karita, Bk. I, 65. Also the Pujawaliya.

M. Burnouf treats these signs very fully; they interested him in two ways; he understood that they illustrated the authenticity of Buddhist classics, evidenced by the concurrence of the records of the Northern and Southern Buddhists, and also considered that they showed the race to which Buddha belonged, some early investigators having supposed that he was a negro, from the fact that some of the idols represented him as having woolly hair.[1]

HIS MANHOOD.

When the Bodhisat reached the age at which it was thought best to choose his wives, all the most beautiful girls in the kingdom were assembled for his inspection. One lovely girl, named Gopa (elsewhere called Yasodharã),[2] came in last, and he at once gave her hundreds and thousands of rings and bracelets. The king's agents were at once sent to the girl's father to demand her hand in marriage for the son. But the father replied: "The young man has lived in luxury and sloth, and my family give their daughters only to men of strength and courage—to those who can wrestle, play the bow and wield the sword."

Other Śākya families made a similar reply, saying: "Our daughters refuse to come near a young milksop." Then a day was appointed on which the young man should show his skill in athletics.

When the appointed day arrived, a vast crowd was

[1] M. Burnouf, App. Lotus de la bonne Loi.

[2] "Her name," says Oldenberg, "seems to have been unknown to the ancient church. Copious inventions of later times first filled up these gaps in various ways."—*Oldenberg*, "*Buddhism.*" *n., p. 101.*

assembled outside the city, and Gautama distanced all competitors in swimming, jumping, running and wrestling. Then came the test of archery, and Ānanda set up a drum, eight miles distant, for a target; another set up one at a distance of sixteen and another at twenty-four miles, while the father of Yasodharā set up another at a still greater distance, and by this drum stood seven palm trees, and beyond them was a demon made of iron.

After the others had tried their skill, Gautama adjusted his arrow, and his shaft passed through the first iron drum, only eight miles away, then through the one which stood sixteen miles away, and thence through the one which stood twenty-four miles away; then passed through the fourth, which was still farther away, tearing also through the seven trees and the iron demon, and then buried itself in the ground.

When he had also proven his superiority in riding horses and elephants, in kicking and other sports, as well as in music, painting, poetry, dancing and similar accomplishments, the beautiful girl was given him. It is said that sixty thousand girls also entered his household, but Yasodharā remained the chief, and she became the mother of his son, Rāhula.[1]

The king then built three palaces for him, one for each season of the year, and in these he was constantly surrounded by his young wives, who danced and sang and played upon many instruments, and he enjoyed all the pleasures of life.

[1] Lalita Vistara, Chap. viii, p. 173 (Rajendralala's version).

THE FOUR VISIONS.

One day the future Buddha wished to go to a pleasure ground, and, ascending his chariot, he went toward the garden. Then the angels thought "the time for his enlightenment is near, let us show him the omens." Accordingly they caused him to see a man wasted by age. And the Bodhisat asked his charioteer what manner of man it was? On being told that old age awaited every human being, he returned in agitation to the palace.

Again in going to the pleasure grounds, he saw a sick man, and learned that disease, too, was the common lot of humanity, and again he returned home.

Afterward, he saw a dead man, and learning that death, also, came to all, he returned in still greater anxiety to the palace.

Still later, as the future Buddha was going out, he saw a man who had abandoned the world, and he asked his charioteer what kind of a man it was who appeared so strangely? "That," replied the servant, "is a mendicant friar," and he then described the advantages of renouncing the world. . . . And that day the future Buddha, cherishing the thought of renunciation, went to the pleasure grounds.

THE GREAT RENUNCIATION.

The Bodhisat after returning to his palace reclined on his couch, while the women, clad in beautiful array, brought their musical instruments, and danced and sang until he fell asleep. Then they laid aside their instruments, and lying down they fell asleep also.

The Bodhisat on waking saw them in disorder, some grinding their teeth and some yawning and muttering in their sleep. Others had their beauty distorted in other ways, and seeing this great change in their appearance he became more and more disgusted.[1] To him the apartment seemed like a charnel house, and he exclaimed: "Of a verity, I am in a graveyard!" and, his mind turning toward those who had renounced the world, he resolved that very day to follow their example.

Then calling his servant, Channa, he ordered his horse to be saddled, and while he was gone the Bodhisat went to the door of his wife's chamber to look upon his child. He saw her sleeping upon a bed covered with jasmine flowers, and resting her hand on the head of the child. Fearing to waken her he did not touch the boy, but said to himself, "I will come back and see him after I have become a Buddha,"[2] and he left the room.

THE ESCAPE.

The horse that was saddled that night was the splendid Kanthaka; he is represented as being thirty feet in length—his coat white and lustrous as a well polished conch shell, and his head black as the black sapphire. "Help me, O Kanthaka! to enter the

[1] Modern poets have violated the Buddhist accounts in painting this revolting picture in very different colors. The Lalita Vistara, the Buddha-karita and other standard works give vivid descriptions of a scene which is here so lightly touched. Some authors claim that the effect upon his vision was produced by the gods.

[2] The Maha-vagga gives no account whatever of his home-leaving, and perhaps there is no historic basis for either of these pictures.

class of mendicants this very night," exclaimed Gautama, and the horse neighed with delight.

He then mounted, and while Channa held on to the tail of the animal the four guardians of the world held lotus flowers, one under each of the horse's feet. The gates were opened by unseen hands, and Gautama went on his way, with angels in front of him, carrying sixty thousand torches, while others were behind him, and still others were upon either hand.

Advancing thus he passed that night beyond three kingdoms, and arrived at the bank of the river which was thirty leagues away. He would have gone farther, but the horse could not make his way through the mass of flowers, of winged creatures and snakes, which were showered down from Indra's heaven in honor of Gautama's departure. At the bank of the river he signaled his horse, and Kanthaka immediately sprang over it to the opposite bank, five or six hundred yards away. It was here that he dismissed his servant, and bade him take the horse and return.

Some of the Buddhistic standard works describe a terrible scene at the palace when it was discovered that Gautama had fled. The king was beside himself with grief, and his wife threw herself on the ground in despair. The other women beat themselves and sobbed, crying out, "Where is our husband?"

When Channa returned with the horse, poor Yasodharā suddenly recovered a little strength, and throwing her arms around the neck of the horse, she exclaimed :

"Alone, on my bed, where he was sleeping by my side,
I found myself.
He had abandoned me!
Kanthaka, good horse, whither didst thou take him?
Chandaka, pitiless! Why didst thou not awaken me?
Chandaka, fathers and mothers are honored by all,
Why, then, should a wife be abandoned?
Henceforth, I feel I cannot eat or drink!
My hair shall grow vile and matted!
An unblest thing is the forcible parting of a man
and a woman who love!"

THE GREAT TEMPTATION.

The story of the great temptation with which Māra assailed Gautama under the Bo-tree appears to be one of the many additions which have been made to the legend by later hands. "Wherever in the sacred Pāli texts," says Oldenberg," the attainment of Buddhahood is described, there is not a word spoken of Māra."[1] A few passages in the text narrate distinct encounters with Māra; sometimes they refer to a time not long before and sometimes to a time not long after the attainment of Buddhahood, but not here. The Lalita Vistara, however, gives an eloquent description of the contest of Gautama with the hosts of evil after passing six weeks in exhaustive asceticism.

"Seated cross-legged beneath the Bo-tree, he pronounced this vow: 'Here, on this seat, may my body

[1] Oldenberg, "Buddha, sein Leben, seine Lehre, seine Gemeinde" (Hoey's Trans.), p. 85.

dry up, and my flesh dissolve, if I raise myself from this seat before I attain the Bodhi.'

"The Wicked One commanded Gautama to leave the tree and speak to him. Upon his refusal to do so, the Evil One drew his sword from its scabbard, and called out: 'Rise up, as I order. Obey me, or, like a garden weed, be cut in pieces!'" At the same time spirits of darkness hurled mountains of flames and mighty trees at the Bodhisat. Globes of fire darted through the air, and huge masses of iron, with terrible javelins, which were dipped in poison. With majestic calmness he viewed all of these demon hostilities, and the bolts which were launched at him were changed into beautiful flowers.

In the most solemn manner, he then called to Brahmā and to "all the Buddhas that live at the ten horizons," and smiting the ground until the earth reverberated like a huge vessel of brass, he prayed: "Disperse this crew of Kṛishṇa!"[1]

Immediately the horses, chariots and elephants of the demon army were hurled into the mud, and the mighty warriors dispersed.[2] In Turnour's Singhalese biography, the Madurattha-vilāsinī, Brahmā is also introduced into the conflict, but he flies away in abject terror, with his parasol of universal dominion in his hand, and throws it down on the confines of Sakwala.[3]

[1] In Wilson's version of Rig-veda Sanhita, mention is made of fifty thousand Krishnas, all of whom were black demons. Vol. I, p. 192.

[2] Tibetan version.

[3] Pali Buddhistical Annals, Journal Bengal Asiatic Society. Vol. VII, p. 812.

THE ATTAINMENT OF BUDDHAHOOD.

While still under the Bo-tree, he acquired, in the first watch of the night, the knowledge of the past; in the middle watch, the knowledge of the present, and in the third watch, the knowledge of the "Chain of Causation," which leads to the origin of evil.

"Now, while he was still seated there, the Blessed One thought: 'It is in order to attain this throne of triumph that I have undergone successive births for so long a time; that I severed my crowned head from my neck and gave it away; that I tore out my darkened eyes and gave them away; that I gave, to serve others, such sons as Jāli, such daughters as Kaṇhā Jinā, and such wives as Maddī, the queen. This seat is a throne of triumph for me, and I will not leave it yet.'

"Having spent four weeks by the Bo-tree, he went in the fifth week to the Shepherd's Nigrodha tree, and sat there meditating on the truth.

"Now the evil angel, Māra, grieved that he had not succeeded in conquering him, and then the three[1] daughters of Māra drew near and inquired why he was sad? On being told, they volunteered to conquer the new Buddha, and, assuming the forms of beautiful women, they sought to debase him by using all their lying flatteries and snaky charms.

"Six times they went to him and professed to be his most humble hand-maidens. But the Blessed One

[1] In other works the statement is made that there were sixteen of these fiendish females.

said: 'Depart ye! why strive ye thus?' And then the evil women returned to their father, confessing their inability to conquer him.

"When the Blessed One had spent a week at that spot, he went to the Mućalinda tree. There he remained for a week, and Mućalinda, the snake king, shielded him from the storms by winding his coils around him, and by spreading the folds of his hood over his head. Being thus protected by the king of the cobras, he 'enjoyed the bliss of salvation as if he had been resting in a pleasant chamber, free from all disturbances.'[1]

"Thence he went to the Rājāyatana tree, and there, also, he sat down enjoying the bliss of salvation. And so seven weeks passed away, during which time he experienced no bodily wants, but fed on the joy of meditation."

FIRST CONVERTS.

"At that time two merchants were traveling from Orissa to Central India, with five hundred carts. And an angel, who was a blood relation of theirs, stopped their carts, and moved their hearts to offer food to the Buddha. And they took a rice cake and a honey cake and went up to him, and said: 'Oh, Blessed One, have mercy upon us, and accept this food.' And he took the food, and ate it, and the two brothers became converts. He then took his robe and mendicant bowl, and went on proclaiming his views

[1] The story of his protection by the serpent is told in the early Vinaya texts from the Pali (see Maha-vagga, I, 3, I). Many of the early sculptures also represent him sitting at ease within the folds of the snake.

until, after a time, he went to a palm grove attended by a thousand Arahats."

Still later, the successor of the Buddhas was dwelling in a bamboo grove, when his father, Śuddhodana, heard that his son was there, and he sent a faithful messenger, beseeching him to come back.

RETURN HOME.

When the Buddha received the message, he set out for his old home,[1] attended by twenty thousand mendicants. When he arrived in the city he and his followers begged their bread from door to door.

When the mother of his child heard that he was begging, she opened the window and beheld him, distinguished with the thirty-two characteristic signs and the eighty lesser marks of a Great Being, and she announced to the king the fact that his son was begging bread.

The king was deeply agitated, and going out he remonstrated with his son for thus bringing disgrace upon the family.

"This is our custom," answered the Buddha.

"Not so," said the king, "Our descent is from the royal race, and amongst them all not one chief ever begged his bread."

"This descent of kings is your descent," replied Gautama, "but mine is the succession of the Buddhas, from Dīpankara down to Kassapa. These and

[1] It is said that before this faithful messenger was sent the father had sent out consecutively eleven men, each with a retinue of a thousand attendants, to deliver this message. But one company after another embraced Buddhism, and joined the mendicants, no one of them returning.—*Birth Stories*, p. 119.

thousands of other Buddhas have begged their daily bread and lived on alms."

He then stood in the middle of the street and recited the following verse:

> "Rise up, and loiter not!
> Follow after a holy life!
> Who follows virtue rests in bliss,
> Both in this world and in the next."

When he heard this verse repeated, the king attained to the Fruit of the First Path, and Buddha then repeated the following verse:

> "Follow after a holy life!
> Follow not after sin!
> Who follows virtue rests in bliss,
> Both in this world and in the next."

When the king heard this, he attained to the Fruit of the Second Path, and taking Buddha's bowl he conducted him to the palace, with all his retinue, and served them with savory food. When the meal was over, all the women came and did reverence to Buddha, save the mother of Rāhula, and she waited for him to come to her. When he came she bowed down and held him by the ankles, while the king told the Buddha of her faithfulness. "When my daughter heard," said the king, "that you had put on the yellow robes, she dressed only in yellow, and when she heard of your taking only one meal a day, she adopted the same custom." "It is no wonder, oh, king!" was the reply, "that she should watch over herself, now that she has you for her protector; formerly, even when wandering in the mountains, she watched over herself." And then he told the story of his own birth as a moon-sprite and went away. Afterward the mother of Rāhula told him to go to his father and ask for his inheritance, and when he did so, instead of giving him the wealth for which he asked, Buddha ordered that the boy be received into the Order, and it was done. The king, however, grieved deeply, and besought Buddha that he would never again receive a child into the Order without the consent of his guardians.

THE FIRST MONASTERY.

The first monastery was built by a householder, who bought the grove where it was placed for eighteen koṭis of gold pieces, laying them side by side over the ground, and he built a monastery, which was dedicated "to the Order of Mendicants, with the Buddha at their head, and to all, from every direction, now present or hereafter to come."

It is said that this monastery was built upon the very spot which was purchased for the same purpose in the time of the blessed Buddha Vipassin, and the merchant who then bought it did so by laying golden bricks over it, and then built there a monastery which was a league in length.

And in the time of the blessed Buddha Sikhin, a merchant purchased that very spot by covering it with golden ploughshares, and built there a monastery which was three-fourths of a league in length.

And in the time of the blessed Buddha Vessabhū, a merchant bought the land by laying golden elephant feet along it, and he built a monastery which was half a league in length.

In the time of Buddha Koṇāgamana, a merchant named Ugga bought the site by laying golden tortoises over it; and during the reigns of the other Buddhas other merchants bought it by covering the ground with gold, and built monasteries there, for the place had been consecrated by the presence of all the Buddhas, and therefore Gautama lived there until his death.[1]

[1] Buddhist Birth Stories, Vol. I, pp. 66-132.

CHAPTER IV.

HISTORIC SKETCH OF BUDDHA

THE THEORY OF A MYTH — BIRTH AND EARLY LIFE — ASCETICISM — ENLIGHTENMENT — DISCOURSE AT BENARES — SERMON ON THE NON-EXISTENCE OF THE SOUL — THE FIRE SERMON — RELIEF FROM TRANSMIGRATION — THE FATAL MEAL — THE DEATH OF BUDDHA.

IT is from such material as that contained in the foregoing chapter that scholars have attempted to sift a biography of Buddha which shall be historic in its character. An effort has been made to distinguish between the true and the false by rejecting the impossible. "It is not a safe process, however," says F. Max Müller, "to distill truth out of legend by simply straining it through the sieve of physical possibility. Many things are possible which may yet be the mere inventions of later writers, and many things have been recovered as historical, after removing from them the thin film of mythological phraseology."[1]

In view of all the difficulties of the situation, we can hardly wonder that some critical scholars have despaired of attempting to sift truth from fiction, and have even questioned the existence of Buddha.

[1] F. Max Müller, "Chips." Vol. I, p. 205.

Senart and Kern claim that the story of the life of Buddha was founded upon a solar myth,[1] and Professor Wilson freely expresses his opinion that it is doubtful whether any such man ever existed.

In support of this position, the great Orientalist dwells upon the fact that many different dates[2] are assigned to his birth, and the total variation between them present the enormous discrepancy of more than two thousand years. He shows also that the clan of Śākyas is never mentioned by the early Hindū writers, and dwells upon the fact that all the names of Buddha are allegorical, except Gautama.

Besides the name of Buddha (which means enlightened), he has seventeen other titles or epithets, which are significant of various qualifications, or positions. For instance, one of the most common appellations for him is Śākya-muni (Sage of the tribes of Śākyas), and we have also Śākya-siṉa (Lion of the Śākyas),

[1] Senart claims that the tree under which Buddha received enlightenment was the cloud tree. In the clouds, the heavenly fluid is stored, and it is guarded by dark demons. In the hymns of the Veda, the powers of light and darkness fight their great battle for the clouds, and the water which they contain. This is the identical battle of Buddha, according to the French scholar.

[2] We have in all about thirty different statements on this subject; for instance, the Chinese give the following six dates as the time of his birth: 640, 767, 949, 950 and 1130 B. C.

From Buddhistic works, in Tibet, fourteen different dates have been gathered by Csoma de Körös, and they are as follows: 546, 576, 653, 752, 837, 880, 882, 884, 1060. 1310, 2135, 2139, 2144 and 2422 B. C.

In India we have the following different dates, which were collected by a Chinese pilgrim named Hiouen-thsang; 260, 360, 560, 660 and 860 B. C.

In Ceylon the official date is 1077 B. C. (Laidlay's Pilgrimage of Fa Hian). Japan furnishes still another, as the Japanese claim that he was born 1000 B. C.

Thus we have twenty-seven dates, with a variation of more than two thousand years between them, besides the various opinions of modern authorities.

and many others. He claims that, not only are the names of Buddha allegorical, but also the names of those connected with him, the name of his father signifying "he whose food is pure," while his mother's name signifies "illusion." Wilson maintains, too, that Kapilavastu, which has been called the birthplace of Buddha, is unknown to Hindū geography, and suggests that it may be rendered "the substance of Kapila." He apparently understands that reference is here made to the doctrines of Kapila, upon which some scholars suppose the principal theories of Buddha to be founded.

"It seems not to be impossible," he says, "that Śākya-muni is an unreal being, and that all which is related of him is as much fiction as is that of his preceding migrations, and the miracles attending his birth, his life and his departure."[1]

"It is evident," says Oldenberg, "that the narrative concerned may be a myth — the conditions which suffice to make the concoction of such a myth possible certainly exist. And this possibility of a purely mythical conception gains further support by the undoubted mythical character of the occurrences yet to be discussed, which followed the attainment of Buddhahood. But showing that a thing may be a myth is not equivalent to showing that it is a myth, and I am inclined to think that that which can be urged in favor of an opposite conception is not without its weight." He concludes his discussion of this subject by an expression of his belief that "in the narrative

[1] Wilson. Essay on Buddha and Buddhism.

of how the Śākya youth became the Buddha, there is really an element of historical memory."[1]

To reject everything which has been written of him appears as unreasonable as to believe it all, and it seems not impossible to gather a few historic facts from the mass of legends connected with him; and hence, we give the following outline, which is correct, so far as it can be gathered from the most authentic sources, although much of it is necessarily legendary, as we are indebted to Hindū authors for information.

BIRTH AND EARLY LIFE.

Allusion has already been made to the multitude of dates[2] which are given by Buddhists themselves concerning the time of Gautama's birth, and there is also considerable uncertainty among critical scholars upon this subject, but the discrepancy here is much smaller, and the best estimates do not vary from each other more than half a century.

We must, therefore, accept about the beginning of the fifth century before Christ as the time of his birth, and the territory of Kośala, about one hundred miles northwest of Benares, as his earliest home. He was the son of Śuddhodana, who was a land owner of the tribe of Śākyas, and, although certainly not a king, still he may have been a chief of the tribe. His mother's name is called Māya, and she was the wife of Śuddhodana.

Many things have been added in modern times of

[1] Oldenberg, pp. 109-112. [2] See note to p. 64.

which the primitive Buddhists never heard. For instance, we now have the statement that "he was conceived of the Holy Ghost," "born of the Virgin Māya," "song of the heavenly host," "presentation in the temple," "temptation in the wilderness" and other similar expressions, which are unknown to the early Pāli texts. The idea that the writers of the gospels were in any way indebted to Buddha is not entertained by scholars.[1]

If those who are still engaged in the manufacture of these "similarities" will read a portion of the New Testament, it may save them from repeating the blunders of their predecessors, some of whom have asserted that certain things were "borrowed from Buddhism" which are not contained in the gospels at all!

The name of Gautama (which, in Pāli, is spelled Gotama) was given him by his parents, and all others are simply epithets or titles which were applied to him in later years. It is probably true that he was married early in life, as that is still the custom in India. The sons of respectable families in modern times could not remain single after the age of sixteen, or seventeen, without bringing more or less reproach upon themselves and their friends. He doubtless had several wives, but the name of the prin-

[1] In a recent letter to the author, Prof. James Legge writes as follows: "I do not think Christianity is at all indebted to Buddhism. And so far as my knowledge goes, the idea of any such indebtedness is generally repudiated by scholars."

See also Oldenberg, B., p. 115; Rhys Davids, Int. to Tevigga Sutta, p. 165; Ss. Bks. E., Vol. II.

Compare also Sir Monier Monier-Williams, B., p. 541, and various addresses; F. Max Müller, Chips, Vol. I, p. 180; Barthélemy Saint-Hilaire, Membre de le l'Institut, Le Bouddha et sa Religion, Int., p. 7, and others.

cipal one, who is supposed to have been the mother of Rāhula, is not given in the Pāli Piṭakas or early texts.

"Probably this name was unknown to the Buddhists in early times, and thus we may best account for the difference of the simply invented names given to this lady by later writers."[1]

It is claimed that Rāhula, the only son, was not born until the father was twenty-nine years of age, at which time he was becoming convinced of the vanity of amusements and was contemplating the idea of entering upon a monastic life.

ASCETICISM.

The story of the four visions is surely reasonable enough if we divest it of the features of supernaturalism. Although we might not accept the statement that these scenes were created by the gods, still it would be easy to suppose that Gautama might see an old man, and a man who was worn by disease; that he might also meet a funeral procession, and see a monk, is not improbable, but we have no proof that these things influenced him in his course.

Oldenberg says of the story of the four visions that "it was a legend which was narrated of one of the legendary Buddhas of by-gone ages, and it was transferred to the youth of Gautama."[2]

It is apparently true that he left his home, and

[1] Rhys Davids and Oldenberg. See their notes to the English translation of the Maha-vagga, I, 542. Also Rhys Davids, B., p. 50, and Oldenberg, B., p. 101.

[2] Oldenberg, B., p. 103.

wife and child, and became the disciple of two Brāhmans, who taught him their own philosophy. It is supposed that the connection between Buddhism and Brāhmanism may be due to the ideas which Gautama here learned of the priesthood. But he failed to find here the peace which he sought, and his thoughts turned to one of the favorite theories of Brāhmanism—the doctrine that self-inflicted bodily suffering is most efficacious for the accumulation of religious merit. The devotees of this idea sometimes sat all day during the hottest months surrounded by five fires, or with four fires around them and the blazing sun over their heads for the fifth. The gods are represented as performing the most severe austerities in order that they might not be excelled by mortals, for, according to the Hindū theory, even the gods might be supplanted by the power which men could acquire by a protracted endurance of bodily suffering.

Gautama, therefore, sought the company of five other ascetics, and began his celebrated fast. Sitting down, unsheltered from the heat of the sun, he gradually reduced his daily allowance of food to a single grain of rice. Then, holding his breath, he macerated his body, and resorted to other means of self-punishment in vain, for he found no peace of mind. Then he arose from his position and took food and nourishment as before, thereby incurring the disapproval of his companions, who continued their painful austerities. He afterward took his seat under a sacred fig tree (the *Ficus religiosa*, known as the Pippala, or

Pīpal), and gave himself up to other forms of meditation.

ENLIGHTENMENT.

It was under this Bo-tree that he finally attained to that state of mind which is called "perfect enlightenment. Oldenberg claims that it is "a later cast of the tradition," which here inserts an account of the great temptation, the story not having been given in the sacred Pāli texts.[1]

The "true knowledge," which was there evolved, appears to have been the outcome of a single thought. It was the doctrine that the present life is only one link in a chain of countless transmigrations — that existence of any kind involves suffering, and that humanity can only be delivered from suffering by the extinction of all desire, especially the desire for existence. The self which he endeavored to renounce was the self of personality. The self-love which Buddhism deprecates is that which consists in craving for continuous life. Gautama, therefore, took refuge from the troubles of life by breaking all its ties and suppressing all its affections.

The internal self-enlightenment,[2] which is the distinguishing feature of Buddhism, is said to have found its first expression in the utterance of the following sentiment: "Through countless births have I wan-

[1] Oldenberg, B., p. 115.

[2] The Bhagavad-gita asserts that "the sage (Yogi), who is internally happy, internally at peace, and internally illuminated, attains extinction in Brahma." "This," says Williams, "is pure Buddhism, if we substitute cessation of individual existence for Brahma." (See B., p. 38.)

dered, seeking, but not discovering, the maker of this, my mortal dwelling-house, and still, again and again, have birth and life and pain returned. But now, at length, thou art discovered, thou builder of this house. No longer shalt thou rear a house for me. Rafters and beams are shattered, and with the destruction of desire, deliverance from a repeated life is gained at last."[1]

Another struggle awaited him before he decided to publicly advocate his views, being tempted to rest in the inaction, which seems to be the Hindū ideal of happiness. It is said, however, that the god, Brahmā, appeared to him, and admonished him to preach the doctrine.

DISCOURSE AT BENARES.

Instead of the life of perfect indolence, therefore, which he himself advocated, he went out to preach the doctrine; first, to five mendicants who were at the Deer forest in Benares. The following is the substance of the first discourse, as given by the Mahāvagga.

"There are two extremes, O monks! to be avoided by one who has given up the world. A life devoted to sensual pleasures, which is degrading, and a life given to self-mortification, which is profitless. There is a middle path — the noble eight-fold path discovered by the Buddha, which leads to wisdom, to perfect enlightenment, to final extinction of desire and suffering." He also expounded "the four noble truths"

[1] Dhamma-pada, 153, 154.

which were the key to his doctrine, and these may be briefly stated thus:

1st. "All existence—that is, existence in any form, whether on earth or in the heavenly spheres, necessarily involves pain and suffering.

2d. "All suffering is caused by lust, or craving, or desire of three kinds; either for sensual pleasure, for wealth, or for existence.

3d. "Cessation of suffering is simultaneous with extinction of lust, craving and desire.

4th. "Extinction of lust, craving and desire, and cessation of suffering are accomplished by perseverance in the noble eight-fold path, viz.: Right belief or views, right resolve, right speech, right work, right livelihood, right exercise or training, right mindfulness and right mental concentration. And how is all life suffering?

"Birth is suffering, decay is suffering, illness is suffering. Death is suffering. Association with objects we hate is suffering. Separation from objects we love is suffering. Clinging to the five elements of existence is suffering. Complete cessation of thirst and desires is cessation of suffering. This is the noble truth of suffering.

"Thus the Blessed One spoke. The five Bikkhus were delighted, and they rejoiced at the words of the Blessed One. And when this exposition was propounded, the venerable Koṇḍañña obtained the pure and spotless eye of truth (that is to say, the following knowledge): 'Whatever is subject to origination is subject also to the condition of cessation.'"[1]

[1] Maha-vagga, I. 6. 17. The closing paragraph is frequently repeated in the Maha-vagga whenever the Blessed One preached on any subject.

The significance of this discourse, which brought "the pure and spotless eye of truth" to the hearers, must depend upon the interpretation of the word "right" in the description of the eight-fold path. "The explanation," says Williams, "is, that 'right belief' means believing in Buddha and his doctrine; 'right resolve' means abandoning one's wife and family; 'right speech' is recitation of Buddha's doctrine; 'right work' is that of a monk; 'right livelihood' is living by alms as a monk does; 'right exercise' is suppression of the individual self; 'right mindfulness' is keeping in mind the impurities and impermanence of the body; 'right mental concentration' is trance-like quietude."[1] It will be noted that in describing the misery of life, associations with those we love are not mentioned as compensating, in any way, for the occasional presence of those who may be offensive in their personality.

SERMON ON THE NON-EXISTENCE OF THE SOUL.

It was also at Benares, and to the same five monks, that Buddha, a few days later, is represented as saying:

"Mendicants: In whatever way the different teachers regard the soul, they think it is the five skandhas, or one of the five. Thus, mendicants, the unlearned, the unconverted man, who does not associate either with the converted or the holy, or understand their law or live according to it; such a man regards the soul, either as identical with, or as possessing, or as

[1] Williams, B., p. 44.

containing, or as residing in the material properties; or as identical with, or as possessing, or as containing, or as residing in sensation. (The same language is repeated in relation to the other three skandhas, viz.: Ideas, propensities and mind.)

"By regarding the soul in one of these twenty ways, he gets the idea, *'I am.'*

"Then there are the five organs of sense, and mind, and qualities, and ignorance. From sensation, the sensual, unlearned man derives the notions that 'I am,' 'this I exists,' 'I shall be,' 'I shall, or shall not, have material qualities,' 'I shall, or shall not have, or shall be, either with or without ideas.' But now, mendicants, the learned disciple of the converted, having the same five organs of sense, has got rid of ignorance and acquired wisdom; and, therefore, by reason of the absence of ignorance and the rise of wisdom, the ideas 'I am,' 'this I exists,' 'I shall be,' 'I shall, or shall not, have material qualities, 'I shall, or shall not have, or shall be, either with or without ideas,' do not occur to him."[1]

"The belief in self, or soul, was regarded as so distinctly a heresy that two well known words in Buddhist terminology have been coined to stigmatize it. The first of these words means 'heresy of individuality,' the name given to this belief as one of the three primary delusions (the other being doubt, and a belief in the efficacy of rites and ceremonies), which must be abandoned at the very first stage of the path to holiness.

[1] The above extract is from the Sutta Pitaka, and is also found in other works.

"The other is *attavada*, 'the doctrine of soul or self,' and which is the name given to it as a part of the chain of causes, which leads to the origin of evil. It is there classed with sensuality, heresy (as to eternity and annihilation), and belief in the efficacy of rites and ceremonies—as one of the four *upadanas*, which are the immediate causes of birth, decay, death, sorrow, lamentation, pain, grief and despair."[1]

THE FIRE SERMON.

After Buddha had obtained about three thousand followers, he is said to have delivered this celebrated discourse, which was apparently suggested by the sight of a conflagration. According to the Mahā-vagga, it was, in substance, as follows:

"Everything, O monks! is burning. The eye is burning; visible things are burning; the sensation produced by contact with visible things is burning—burning with the fire of lust, enmity and delusion; with birth and decay, death, grief, lamentation, pain, dejection and despair. The ear is burning; sounds are burning; the nose is burning; odors are burning; the tongue is burning; tastes are burning; the body is burning; objects of sense are burning; the mind is burning; thoughts are burning; all are burning with the fires of passion and lusts. Observing this, O monks! a wise and noble disciple becomes weary or disgusted with the world, weary of things, weary of the ear, weary of sounds, weary of odors, weary of tastes, weary of the body, weary of the mind.

[1] Rhys Davids, B., p. 95.

Becoming weary, he frees himself from passions and lusts. When free, he realizes that his object is accomplished, that he has lived a life of restraint and chastity, and that rebirth is ended."[1]

He here compares all life to flame, and teaches that his followers should extinguish the fires of lust and the desire for existence, while he advocates the importance of monkhood and celibacy for the attainment of this end.

A short time before Buddha's death he delivered to his attendants the following discourse:

RELIEF FROM TRANSMIGRATION.

"And the Blessed One proceeded with a great company of the brethren to Bhaṇḍa-gāma. There the Blessed One addressed them, and said: 'It is through not understanding and grasping the four truths, O brethren! that we have had to run so long, to wander so long, in this weary path of transmigration—both you and I.

"'And what are these four? The noble conduct of life, the noble earnestness of meditation, the noble kind of wisdom, and the noble salvation of freedom. But when noble conduct is realized and known, when noble meditation is realized and known, when noble wisdom is realized and known, when noble freedom is realized and known—then the craving for new existence, *which leads to renewed existence, is destroyed, and there is no more birth.*'"[2]

Before his death he repeatedly alluded to the ap-

[1] Maha-vagga, I. 21. [2] Maha-Parinibbana Sutta, chap. iv, 2.

proaching event as "the final extinction of the Tathāgata[1] (or Buddha), and he frequently spoke of passing away, "by that utter passing away, in which nothing whatever remains behind."[2]

In some of his last addresses he seemed to contradict his life-long teaching, by urging his followers to work out their own salvation from continued transmigration, without looking for help to any one else, not even to Buddha himself.

Although the formula for admission, not only to the monkhood, but also to lay membership, had long been a declaration that the candidate took refuge in Buddha, in the Dhamma (or law), and in the Order, and although this formula is still used in connection with the ceremony of initiation,[3] still we find the Buddha, before his death, addressing the monks as follows: "Be lamps unto yourselves, be a refuge unto yourselves. Betake yourselves to no external refuge. Hold fast to the truth as a lamp. Look not for refuge to any one besides yourselves."[4]

THE FATAL MEAL.

In relation to the events connected with his death, and immediately preceding that event, we apparently come very near to historic ground, as we have the Mahā-parinibbāna-Suttana, or Book of the Great Decease, which is supposed to have come into being

[1] Maha-Parinibbana Sutta, chap. iii, 47, 63, 66.
[2] Ibid, chap. iv, 57; also chap. v, 20, 21.
[3] This formula was used in connection with other matter at the initiation of a candidate into the Buddhist Church in Chicago in 1893.
[4] Maha-Parinibbana Sutta, chap. ii, 33.

not more than a hundred years after Buddha's death. At this time there may well have been reliable traditions concerning the events which took place on his last journey, and this being true, they were probably collected and handed down orally, from one generation to the next, until they were committed to writing at a much later date. From this valuable authority, therefore, we quote as follows:

"At Pāvā the Blessed One stayed at the Mango grove of *K*unda, who was by family a smith. And *K*unda, the worker in metals, . . . addressed the Blessed One, and said: 'May the Blessed One do me the honor of taking his meal, together with the brethren, at my house to-morrow?' And the Blessed One signified by silence his consent. Now, at the end of night, *K*unda, the worker in metals, made ready in his dwelling place sweet rice and cakes and a quantity of dried boar's flesh. And the Blessed One robed himself early in the morning, and, taking his bowl, went with the brethren to the dwelling place of *K*unda. And when he was seated he addressed *K*unda, the worker in metals, and said: 'As to the dried boar's flesh you have made ready, serve me with it, *K*unda; and as to the sweet rice and cakes, serve the brethren with it.' 'Even so, lord!' said *K*unda, the worker in metals, in assent to the Blessed One. And the dried boar's flesh he had made ready he served the Blessed One; whilst the other food . . . he served to the members of the Order.

"Now the Blessed One addressed *K*unda, and said: 'Whatever dried boar's flesh is left over to thee,

*K*unda, that bury in a hole. I see no one on earth, nor in Māra's heaven, nor in Brahmā's heaven, no one among gods and men, by whom, when he had eaten it, that food can be assimilated save by the Tathāgata.' 'Even so, lord,' said *K*unda. And whatever dried boar's flesh was left over, that he buried in a hole.

"Now when the Blessed One had eaten the food prepared by *K*unda, there fell upon him a dire sickness, the disease of dysentery, and sharp pain came upon him, even unto death. But the Blessed One, mindful and self-possessed, bore it without complaint."

The Buddha did not immediately die of his painful ailment, and before passing away he exonorated *K*unda from all blame in the matter.

"And the Blessed One said: 'Now it may happen, Ānanda, that some one should stir up remorse in *K*unda, the smith, . . . in that when the Tathāgata had eaten his last meal from *K*unda's provision, then he died. Any such remorse, Ānanda, should be checked by saying: 'This is good to thee, *K*unda, and gain to thee, in that when the Tathāgata had eaten his last meal from thy provision, then he died.'"

"The offering of food, which when a Tathāgata has eaten, he attains to supreme and perfect insight, and the offering of food, which when a Tathāgata has eaten, he passes away, by that utter passing away, in which nothing whatever remains behind . . . these two offerings of food are of equal fruit and equal profit, and of much greater fruit and much greater profit than any others."[1]

1 Maha-Parinibbana-Sutta, chap. iv.

THE DEATH OF BUDDHA.

After about forty-five year's of itineracy, the death of Buddha took place, probably a little more than four hundred years before Christ.[1]

The body of Buddha was cremated, and the remains were divided into eight portions, one of which was assigned to each of the parties claiming it. Over each portion of the relics a mound was built and a feast was held.

It is probable that in this Sutta, we have much of history, not only because it is one of the oldest of the Buddhist works, but because it records events which would not have been allowed to make their appearance as fiction.

"The external features of this narrative," says Dr. Oldenberg, "bear for the most part, though not in every particular, the stamp of trustworthy tradition."[2] Rhys Davids, Williams and others have called atten-

[1] There is quite a difference of opinion concerning the exact date of his death. Of course there must be as much divergence here as there is in relation to his birth (see note to p. 64), and even among scholars the variation is considerable.

Some years ago it was claimed by such men as Burnouf, Lassen, Wilson and Barthélemy Saint-Hilaire that Buddha's death occurred about 543 B. C., which is an earlier date than is now assigned to his birth. But the latest researches of European scholarship, making use of the inscriptions upon coins, rocks and columns, besides other data, make it much later.

Cunningham is of the opinion that it occurred about 478 B. C., while Prof. F. Max Müller speaks of 477 as "the most plausible date." (See Chips, Vol. I, p. 202.)

Professor Williams thinks it is still later, and assigns 420 "as a round number," although he says that Rhys Davids has good reasons for assigning the event to a later date than this.

Oldenberg and Rhys Davids place the date of his decease at "about 420 — to 400 B. C., or possibly a year or two later."—*Sa. Bks. E., Vol. II, p. 17.*

Kern gives 388 as the most probable date.

[2] Oldenberg, B., p. 196.

tion to the fact that it is extremely improbable that the followers of Buddha should fabricate a story that he died in consequence of eating too freely of pork, in view of the fact that he had always forbidden the killing of animals. Buddhism required even the straining of water, lest one should inadvertently destroy life, and the throwing of water upon grass was forbidden for the same reason. Many animals, including the pig, were held to be especially sacred, because the Buddha was supposed to have occupied such forms during a multitude of previous births, as will be seen by the following chapter.

CHAPTER V.

TEACHINGS OF BUDDHISM.

TRANSMIGRATION — FORMER BIRTHS OF BUDDHA — THE JĀTAKAS—THE ORTHODOX BELIEF — VARIOUS FORMS ASSUMED — THE MONKEYS AND THE DEMON — THE WILY ANTELOPE — THE BULL WHO WON THE BET — THE FISH AND HIS WIFE — THE WISE JUDGE.

THE doctrine of transmigration is much older than Buddhism, and Herodotus affirms that it originated in Egypt, where the people believed that when the body of any one died, the soul entered into some other creature which was born to receive it. They supposed that when it had gone the round of all created forms, on land, in water and in air, it entered once more into the human body which had been born for it. This cycle of existence for the soul was believed to take place once in three thousand years.[1] It is well known that the Egyptians have, for many centuries, exercised great care in the preservation of their dead. They believe that if a limb is broken from a mummy that the soul will be crippled in the same way; and probably the Egyptian custom of embalming the bodies of cats, crocodiles, bulls and some other animals, originated in the idea that they had

[1] Herodotus, ii, 123.

been inhabited by souls, that might, some day, again claim these bodies for their own. This theory of transmigration took early root in Indian soil. It is openly taught in the first of the series of Upanishads,[1] and the germs of these doctrinal works are found in the early songs of the Ṛig-veda, which reach back in the world's history almost to the time of the birth of Moses.[2]

In the early Vedic hymns, however, there appears to be no regular system of either religion or mythology, the doctrines of Brāhmanism being elucidated in later productions. And in these later works a three-fold alternative is presented to the soul; it may pass through deities, through men, or through beasts and plants, according to the degree of merit in the individual, the lowest degree in transmigration being either a vegetable or a mineral. But the souls which have passed even into these lowest forms may afterward ascend through various insects, fish, reptiles, snakes, tortoises and other similar bodies.[3]

All the theories, however, of the Egyptian and Brāhman, require the existence of a soul which passes from one form to another. It was reserved for Buddhism to teach a system of transmigration from one body to another, even while ignoring the existence of a conscious entity. In order to serve the cause of

[1] According to the chronology usually received by Sanskrit scholars, the most ancient of these works slightly preceded the rise of Buddhism, and found their origin five hundred years or more before Christ.

[2] The original composition of the earliest songs of the Rig-veda is assigned to the time between 1500 and 1000 B. C. (See Max Müller, Sir Monier Williams, Kennedy, Stevenson, Wilson, Barthélemy St. Hilaire and others.)

[3] Manu, I, 2-40.

morality, Buddha retained the idea of personal identity, and he therefore established a new connection between individuals in the chain of existence, which he acknowledged by the new assertion that the thing which made two beings to be the same was not soul, but karma. The peculiarity of this teaching is, that the result of what a man is, or does, is held to be concentrated in the formation of a new sentient being; new in its constituent parts and powers, but the same in its essence, its being, its doing, its karma!

The theory is that as soon as a man, animal or angel dies, a new being is produced, in a more or less painful state of existence, according to the karma—the desert or merit—of the being who died.[1] Rebirth as an animal, that is to say, the transfer of a man's karma to an animal, clearly forms a part of the oldest Buddhist belief; and the authors of later works rightly take it for granted.

"The curious doctrine of transmigration satisfied the unfortunate that their present woes were the result of their actions in a former birth, and would be avoided in future existences by liberality to the priests in the present life."[2]

FORMER BIRTHS OF BUDDHA.

In the Cariyā Piṭaka, which is included in the supplementary part of the Pāli Piṭakas, the karma of Buddha is represented to have belonged, and apparently in succession, to both men and animals. It is clear

[1] See Rhys Davids, "Origin and Growth of Religion," pp. 93, 107. Also "Buddhism," pp. 24, 101, 104.

[2] Ibid, p. 24.

that, during his long period of transmigration from one form to another, some identity must have been retained if he could remember the various acts and emotions of his former lives. He is represented as not only remembering his early experiences, but also of repeating various portions of his pre-existent history for the instruction and edification of his hearers. Not only this, but one of the early Suttas records his teaching to the effect that, by a certain mode of life, his hearers would be able to call to mind their various temporary conditions in the ages gone by. "Such as one birth, two births, three, four, five, ten, twenty . . . a hundred, a thousand, or an hundred thousand births. 'In that place,' he would then be able to say, 'such was my name, my family, my caste, my experience of comfort or of pain, and such the limit of my life. And when I passed from thence, I took form again in that other place . . . and when I fell from thence, I took form in such and such a place.' "[1]

Many of the Buddha's experiences in former births are given in

THE JĀTAKAS.

"The Buddhist scriptures are sometimes spoken of as consisting of nine different divisions, of which the seventh is the 'Jātakas,' or 'The Jātaka Collection.' This division of the sacred books is mentioned, not only in the Dīpava*m*sa itself and in the Sumaṇgala

[1] Asankheyya-Sutta, 17. This teaching is apparently as authentic as anything in the whole line of this literature, as it is not only found in this Sutta, but the text of this clause occurs nearly word for word in the Brahma-jala Sutta, pp. 17-21. Also in the Lalita Vistara, chap. xxii, p. 442. It also occurs exactly in the Samanna Phala Sutta, p. 148. (*Sa. Bks. E., Vol. XI, p. 216.*)

Vilāsinī, but also the Aṇguttara Nikāya (one of the later works included in the Pāli Piṭakas), and in the Saddharma Puṇḍarīka (a late but standard work of the Northern Buddhists). It is common, therefore, to both of the two sections of the Buddhist Church; and it follows that it was probably in use before the great schism took place, possibly before the Council of Vesāli.[1] In any case it is important evidence of the existence of a collection of Jātakas at a very early date."[2]

Among the most interesting and important archaeological discoveries which have recently been made in India are those of the Buddhist carvings on the railings and around the dome-shaped shrines of Amaravatī, Sānchi and Bharhut. There have been found figures boldly cut in deep bas-relief which prove to be illustrations of the sacred Birth Stories—scenes from the life of Gautama in his various births, and also illustrations of the well-known Buddhist theory that, at the time of his conception, he entered his mother's side in the form of a white elephant. These bas-reliefs afford indisputable evidence in relation to the age of the Jātaka stories, for it proves that they were already, at the end of the third century before Christ, considered so sacred that they were chosen as subjects to be represented around the most sacred Buddhist buildings. It is also demonstrated that they were popularly

[1] The Council of Vesali was held about one hundred years after the death of Buddha, to settle disputes as to points of discipline and practice which had arisen in the Order. The hundred years is a "round number," but it is supposed that the council was held within thirty years of 350 B. C. (See "Birth Stories," Vol. I, Int. p. 56.)

[2] Ibid, Int. p. 62.

known as "Jātakas," by the inscription over a number of the carvings on the railing at Bharhut.[1]

THE ORTHODOX BELIEF.

"The belief of orthodox Buddhists on the subject is that the Buddha was accustomed to explain and comment upon things which happened around him, by telling of similar events which had occurred in his own previous births. The experience, not of one lifetime, but of many lives, was always present in his mind. The stories thus told are said to have been reverently learned and repeated by his disciples, and immediately after his death five hundred and fifty of them were gathered together in one collection, called the 'Book of Five Hundred and Fifty Jātakas or Births.' . . . The commentary to this work gives for each story an account of the event in Gautama's life which led to the telling of that particular story. Both text and commentary were then handed down intact in the Pāli language, in which they were composed, until the time of the Council of Patna.[2] They were carried in the following year to Ceylon, where the commentary was translated into Singhalese, and in the fifth year of our era retranslated in its present form in the Pāli language. But the text of the Jātaka stories themselves has been throughout preserved in its original Pāli form."

"Unfortunately," continues Rhys Davids, "this orthodox belief, as to the history of the book, rests

1 B. B. S., Vol. I, Int. pp. 59–69.

2 The Council of Patna is supposed to have been held about the year 250 B. C.

upon a foundation of quicksand. The Buddhist belief that most of their sacred books were in existence immediately after Buddha's death is not only not supported, but is contradicted by the evidence of the books themselves."[1]

Still, it is highly probable that all those Birth Stories, which are not only found in the Jātaka book itself, but are also referred to in other parts of the Pāli Piṭakas, are at least older than the Council of Vesāli.

In thus ascribing an early origin to any portion of the literature of India, we must rid ourselves of the thought that it could only exist in written form, as it was, for centuries, the custom of that people to pass their sacred books from one generation to the next, by repetition from the lips of their priests. As they form a portion of the most sacred of the Buddhist scriptures, being even now daily repeated to eager listeners in every Buddhist country, and are believed by the orthodox to be veritable history, the Jātakas are well worthy of examination, and a few of them will be given in the present chapter.

VARIOUS FORMS ASSUMED.

It is said there have been five hundred and fifty different births,[2] concerning which anecdotes have come down to us, and in some of the Buddhist temples, it is claimed, there are relics of Gautama in the

[1] B. B. S. Int. pp 1, 2.

[2] Five hundred and fifty is a round number, both in relation to the stories and the number of births. There are many more of the tales, and in some of them there are two consecutive births of Buddha, while, at times, several stories are told of the same birth.

shape of hair, feathers and other fragments of the different creatures whose bodies he previously wore.

According to Buddhist authorities, Gautama was born once each as a fairy, a hare, a frog, a waterfowl, a carpenter, a devil dancer, a silversmith, a gambler, a curer of snake bites, and a dog. He was born eighty-three times as an ascetic and eighty-five times as a king. Twice he was born as a pig, twice as a thief, twice as a rat, and also repeatedly lived the life of a jackal, a fish, a woodpecker and a crow. He was born forty-three times as a tree-god, and twenty-four times as a Brāhman. In twenty-six lives he was a teacher, in twenty-four he was a courtier, and he also led twenty-four lives as a king's son. In three lives he was an outcast, and in three forms of existence a potter. Four times he was born a peacock, four times he was the god Brahmā; in four lives, also, he was a horse, and four times a bull. In twenty-three lives he was a nobleman, and in twenty-two a learned man. Five times he was born an eagle, and five times a slave. Six times he was an elephant, and six times a snipe. Eight times he lived as a wild duck, and ten times he led the life of a lion. Eleven times he was a deer, and twelve times a man of property. Thirteen of his lives were devoted to commerce, but eighteen times he was a monkey.[1]

"The noteworthy point," says Sir M. Monier-Williams, "about the repeated births of Buddha, is that there has been no Darwinian rise from lower to higher forms, but a mere jumble of metamorphoses."[2]

[1] B. B. S., p. cl. [2] Williams, B., p. III.

It is true that he is represented as being born in the Tusita heavens the last time before he was born on earth; but, says Oldenberg, "this in no way implies that a superhuman nature is claimed for him. One who is a god in one existence may, in the next existence, be born as an animal, or he may be born in hell."[1]

Although Buddha passed many lives in the humble forms of the frog, the snipe, the rat, the fish, the serpent, the monkey, and others of a similar character — though he repeatedly led the life of a thief, an outcast and a gambler, still he escaped the greatest degradation to which he could have been subjected in the eyes of the people of India, in that he was never born a woman!

THE MONKEYS AND THE DEMON.

This is a story which was told by the Teacher when he was living at the Ketaka wood. It was here that the novices brought canes to the monks for needle cases, and, finding them hollow throughout, they went to the Teacher and inquired of him how it happened that the Na*l*a-canes were hollow from root to point. "This, mendicants," said he, "is a former command of mine." And then he told the tale as follows:

"There was formerly a lake in which there was a water demon, who used to eat whomsoever went down into the water. At that time the Bodhisat was a monkey king, as large as the fawn of a red deer, and he was attended by a troop of about eighty thousand monkeys. He preserved them from harm, and he said

[1] Oldenberg, B., p. 324.

to them one day: 'My children! in this forest there are poisonous trees, and pools which are haunted by demons. When you are going to eat fruit which you have not eaten before, or to drink where you have not drunk before, ask me about it.'

"They answered in accordance with his wishes, and one day when searching for water, they found a pool, but sat down and awaited his arrival before drinking.

"He then examined the shores of the pond, and saw the marks of footsteps which went down into the pond, but he found none which came back. Then he knew it was haunted by demons, and he said: 'My children! you have done well in not drinking this water, for the pond is haunted!' Then the demon of the water, seeing that they were not coming in, came splashing through the water in horrible shape, and commanded them to come down and drink the water.

"The Bodhisat refused to do so, and said: 'I suppose you think we must go down to drink. But you are wrong! Each one of us eighty thousand shall take a Na*l*a-cane and drink the water from your pond without ever entering it, as easily as one would drink from the hollow stem of a water plant, so you will have no power to eat us!'"

It was when the Teacher, as Buddha, had recalled this circumstance that he uttered the following stanza:

"I saw the marks of feet that had gone down,
I saw no marks of feet that had returned;
We'll drink the water through a reed,
And yet I'll not become your prey."

So saying, the Bodhisat had a Na*la*-cane brought to him, and appealing in great solemnity to the Ten Great Perfections[1] exercised by him in this and previous births, he blew into the cane, and the cane became hollow throughout, not a single knot being left in it. Then the Bodhisat walked round the pond saying: "Let all the canes growing here be perforated throughout." And thenceforth, since, through the greatness and goodness of the Bodhisat, his commands are fulfilled, all the canes which grew in that pond became perforated throughout.

After giving this command, the Bodhisat took a cane and seated himself, and the other monkeys (eighty thousand in number) each took one, and drawing the water up into their canes, they all sat safely on the bank while drinking. When the Teacher had finished his discourse on the hollowness of the canes, he added: "He who was then the water demon was Deva-datta; the eighty thousand monkeys were the Buddha's retinue; but the monkey king, clever in resource, was I myself."[2]

"Long ago, in the fifth dispensation before the present one, the Bodhisat was a dealer in brass and tinware in a country called Servia. He here went from house to house buying up old metals, and it was here that he incurred the hatred of a rival dealer (who was afterward born as Deva-datta), by buying a

[1] Generosity, morality, self-denial, wisdom, perseverance, patience, truth, resolution, kindness and resignation.

[2] This is the Nala-pana Jataka, and it is probably the one which is illustrated by the Bharhut sculptor in the scene where he has represented many monkeys sitting down and listening to the discourse of the Bodhisat.

golden dish which the other hawker had temporarily refused for the purpose of getting it cheaper.

When Gautama was living as the Buddha, and this man had been born as Deva-datta, he became a Buddhist, but on one occasion he asked for the Five Rules, and failing to get them, he made a schism in the Order, and taking four hundred of the mendicants with him, went and dwelt elsewhere. And hence his enmity for Buddha had obtained through the long ages of many births.

THE WILY ANTELOPE.

This story is told by the Teacher about Deva-datta while they were at Jetavana. The monks sat talking in the lecture hall of the wickedness of him who, they said, was seeking to slay the Sage. "Not only now, O mendicants!" said the Teacher, "has Deva-datta gone about to slay me; he formerly did the same and was unsuccessful." "Once upon a time," he continued, "the Bodhisat became an antelope, and lived in his forest home, feeding upon fruits, and at one time he went often to a certain heavily laden tree. A deer stalker in the village near by, noted the tracks of the deer at the foot of the tree, and after an early breakfast he climbed the tree with his javelin and waited for his game. The Bodhisat, too, left his lair early in the morning, and came up to eat the fruits; but, instead of going hastily to the tree, he thought to himself: 'The hunters are sometimes in the trees; I wonder if there can be any danger of that kind?' And he stopped at a distance. Seeing him hesitate the hunter cautiously threw some fruit toward him. Then, looking up, the Bodhisat saw the hunter, but pretending not to see him he called out: 'O tree! you have been wont to let your fruit fall straight down, but to-day you have given up your tree nature, so I shall go and seek my food elsewhere.' Then the angry hunter hurled his javelin after him, exclaiming: 'Away with you—I have lost you this time!' The Bodhisat turned around and replied: 'O man! I tell you that, though you have lost me this time, you have not lost the eight great hells and the sixteen Ussada hells, and five-fold bondage and torment—the result of your conduct. These you have not lost.'"

And when the Teacher had finished this discourse, he added these words: "He who was then the hunter was Deva-datta, but the antelope was I myself."[1]

THE BULL WHO WON THE BET.

There were six bad monks whose evil deeds and words are said to have given occasion for many a by-law which was enacted in the Vinaya Piṭaka for the guidance of the Buddhist order of mendicants. And on one occasion, the six made a disturbance by scorning, snubbing and annoying peaceable monks, and overwhelming them with the ten kinds of abuse. Buddha reproved the refractory monks, saying: "Harsh speaking, O mendicants! is unpleasant even to animals. An animal once made a man lose a thousand

[1] B. B. S., p. 237.

who addressed him harshly. Long ago, in the reign of King Gandhāra, the Bodhisat came to life as a bull. The bull's name was Nandi Visāla, and the owner was very fond of it, feeding it on gruel and rice. The animal became very strong, and one day he said to his owner: 'Go now to some rich squire, rich in cattle, and offer to bet him a thousand that your ox will move a hundred laden carts.' The Brāhman did so, and the cattle owner readily took the bet; whereupon the owner of Nandi Visāla filled an hundred carts with sand and gravel stones, ranged them all in a row, and tied them firmly together. Then he bathed the ox, gave him a measure of scented rice, hung a garland around his neck, and yoked him by himself to the front cart. Then he took his seat on the pole, raised his goad aloft, and called out: 'Gee up, you brute! Drag 'em along, you wretch!' The Bodhisat said to himself: 'He calls me a wretch. I am no wretch!' and he stood perfectly still. Then the squire claimed his bet, and the Brāhman was compelled to pay him a thousand pieces, after which he went home overwhelmed with grief. Afterward Nanda Visāla said to his master: 'I have lived long in your house; have I ever done any harm?' And the Brāhman answered: 'Never.' 'Then why did you call me a wretch? Your loss is your own fault. It's not my fault. Go now and bet him two thousand, and never call me a wretch again—I who am no wretch at all!'

"So the Brāhman went and bet two thousand, and the carts were tied together as before, and when all was ready the Brāhman seated himself on the pole, stroked Nandi Visāla on the back, and called out: 'Gee up, my beauty! Drag it along, my beauty!'

"And the Bodhisat with one mighty effort dragged forward the hundred heavily laden carts, and brought the hindmost one up to where the foremost one had formerly stood. Then the cattle owner acknowledged himself beaten, and handed over the two thousand pieces to the Brāhman. The bystanders also gave a large sum to the Bodhisat, and the whole became the property of the Brāhman."

After repeating this circumstance the Buddha uttered the following stanza to the six mendicants as a rule of conduct:

"Speak kindly; never speak in words unkind!
He moved a heavy weight for him who kindly spake.
He gained him wealth; he was delighted with him!"

When the Teacher had given them this lesson in virtue, he summed up the Jātaka as follows: "The Brāhman of that time was Ānanda, but Nandi Visāla (the kind bull) was I myself."[1]

THE FISH AND HIS WIFE.

It sometimes happened that after deserting his wife and children to become a member of the order of mendicants, the human heart of the monk hungered for his family, and longed for the company of the loving wife whom he had left. While at Jetavana Buddha learned that one of his followers was thus tempted, and he asked him: "Is it true, then, that you are lovesick?"

[1] B. B. S., p. 266.

"It is true, lord!" was the reply.

"What has made you sad?"

"Sweet is the touch of the hand of her who was formerly my wife. I cannot forsake her!"

"O brother!" said the Teacher, "this woman does you harm. In a former birth, also, you were just being killed through her when I came up and saved you."

When Brahmadatta was reigning in Benares the Bodhisat became his private chaplain. At that time certain fishermen were casting their nets into the river, and a big fish came swimming along with his wife. She was in front of him, and smelling the net she made a circuit and escaped it, but the other went into it. When the fishermen felt him coming in they pulled up the net, seized the fish and threw him alive on the sands, and began to prepare a fire and spit, intending to cook and eat it.

Then the fish lamented, saying to himself: "The heat of the fire would not hurt me, nor the torture of the spit, nor any other pain of that sort; but that my wife should sorrow over me, thinking I must have deserted her for another, that is, indeed, a dire affliction!" And he uttered the following stanza:

"'Tis not the heat, 'tis not the cold,
'Tis not the torture of the net;
But that my wife should think of me,
'He's gone now to another for delight.'"

Just then the chaplain came down, attended by his slaves, to bathe at the ford. And he understood the language of all animals; so hearing the fish's lament, he thought: "This fish is lamenting the lament of sin. Should he die in this unhealthy frame of mind he would assuredly be reborn in hell. I will save him." And he went to the fishermen and said: "My good men, do you not furnish a fish for us every day for our curry?" And they gave him the fish. The Bodhisat took it up in his hands, seated himself on the river side, and said to it: "My good fish! Had I not caught sight of you this day, you would have lost your life. Now, henceforth, sin no more!" And thus exhorting it he threw it into the water and returned to the city.

When the Teacher had finished this discourse he proclaimed the truths, and the depressed monk was established in the fruit of conversion. Then the Teacher made the connection, and summed up the Jātaka: "She who at that time was the female fish was the former wife; the fish was the depressed monk, but the chaplain was I myself."[1]

In striking contrast with the foregoing, we find a story in the same collection which was apparently borrowed from an earlier literature. It appears to be merely an Indian version of the judgment of Solomon recorded in the Book of Kings, which is much older than Buddha. Of course the narrative has received certain characteristic accretions, and Buddha is made the hero, but the similarities are too strong to be ignored by scholars. The facilities for possible borrowing from the older Semitic literature will be discussed in another chapter.[2]

[1] B. B. S., 299. [2] See Chap. X.

THE WISE JUDGE.

"A woman carrying her child, went to the future Buddha's tank to wash. And, having first bathed the child, she descended into the water to bathe herself. Then a Yakshiṇī,[1] seeing the child, had a craving to eat it. And taking the form of a woman she drew near and asked the mother: 'Friend, this is a very pretty child; is it one of yours?' Being told that it was, she asked if she might nurse it. This being allowed, she nursed it a little and then carried it off. But when the mother saw this, she ran after her and caught hold of her, crying out: 'Where are you taking my child?' The Yakshiṇī boldly said: 'It is mine!' And so quarreling, they passed the door of the future Buddha's judgment hall. Hearing the noise, he sent for them, and after inquiring into the matter, he asked if they would abide by his decision.

"They agreed to do so, and he then had a line drawn on the ground, and told the Yakshiṇī to take hold of the child's arms, and the mother to take hold of its legs. 'The child,' said he, 'shall be her's who drags him over the line.'

"But as soon as they pulled at him, the mother, seeing how he suffered, grieved as if her heart would break, and letting him go, she stood there weeping.

"Then the future Buddha asked the bystanders: 'Whose hearts are tender to babes; those who have borne children or those who have not?'

[1] The Yakshas, products of witchcraft and cannibalism, are beings of magical power who feed upon human flesh. The male (Yaksha) occupies in the Buddhist stories a position similar to that of the wicked genius in the Arabian Nights. The female (Yakshini), who occurs more frequently, usually plays the part of a siren.

"And they answered: 'O Sire! the hearts of mothers are tender.'

"'Whom do you think is the mother; she who has the child in her arms or she who has let go?'

"And they answered: 'She who has let go is the mother.'

"'This,' said he (of her who held the child), 'is a Yakshiṇī, who took the child to eat it.'

"'O Sire! How did you know it!'

"'Because her eyes winked not and were red, and she knew no fear and had no pity, I knew it.'

"On being questioned, the Yakshiṇī then confessed her identity and admitted that she took the child to eat it. But the mother exalted the future Buddha, and, praising him, she went away with her child clasped to her bosom."[1]

A limited space forbids the examination of many other interesting stories belonging to this series.

For instance, a story which was told by Buddha at Jetavana while the December festival was being held to celebrate the close of the season called "*was*," or the months of rainy weather. The Buddha had spent "*was*" among the angels, not because he cared to go to heaven for his own sake, but he went in order "to give the angels an opportunity of learning how to forsake the error of their ways."[2]

After remaining some time in heaven, he descended on the day of this great festival; and when the monks were seated in the great lecture hall, they began to

[1] B. B. S. Int. p. 14.

[2] See Professor Cowell in *Indian Antiquary* for 1879.

extol the virtues of the Teacher, saying: "Truly, brethren! unequaled is the power of the Tathāgata. The yoke which the Tathāgata bears, none else is able to bear!" "O mendicants," said the Buddha, "who should now bear the yoke that I can bear? For even when an animal in a former birth, I could find no one to drag the weight which I dragged." He then told them of his experience when he was the old woman's black bull, and his name was "Blackie." It was then that he was enabled to make money for his owner by dragging carts, which were so heavy that not one of them could be moved by five hundred pair of other cattle.[1]

He also told the story of his birth as a wise dog, when he convinced the king that the royal harness had been gnawed by the dogs belonging to the palace, and thereby saved the life of himself and other vagrant dogs that had been accused of the act.[2]

And again he told of his life as a king of the geese, when he rebuked the vanity of a monk who had been born as a dancing peacock.[3]

The fact that many elaborate similes are used to enforce the arguments in the Pāli Suttas would seem to prove that Buddha was accustomed to teach in the way which these stories indicate.

"It is not improbable," says Rhys Davids, "that the compiler was quite correct in attributing to him that subtle sense of humor which led to inventing, as

[1] B. B. S., p. 270. [2] Ibid, p. 240.

[3] Ibid, p. 291. The story of the dancing peacock is one of those which are illustrated by the carvings in bas-relief around the Great Tope at Bharhut. It must, therefore, be very old.

occasion arose, some fable or some tale of previous birth, to explain away existing failures in the conduct of monks or to draw a moral from contemporaneous events."[1]

All animals are more or less venerated under the Buddhist system—indeed, it cannot be otherwise when every Buddhist believes that Buddha himself was incarnated hundreds of times in various animal forms.

As Buddha was a pig in two of his births, and died at last in consequence of eating too freely of pork, even the pig is sacred, and in the sculptures of the Tāntrik goddess Vajra-vārāhī (adopted by Northern Buddhists), a row of seven pigs is carved underneath her, and one of her three heads is that of a pig.

The feeling of reverence for animals, which is so prominent a feature of Buddhism, rests upon the doctrine of metempsychosis. Of course neither Hindū nor Buddhist can draw a line of demarkation between gods, men and animals, when the same living being may exist as a god, a man or an animal. It is on this account that in India animals mingle freely with the natives. "Bulls walk about independently in the streets and jostle you on the pavements; monkeys domesticate themselves on the roof of your house; crows make themselves at home on the window sill and carry off any portable article of jewelry that takes their fancy on your dressing table; sparrows take the bread off your table cloth; swarms of insects claim a portion of your meal; bats career triumphantly about your head in the bedroom, and, at certain seasons, snakes domi-

[1] Rhys Davids, Ibid, p. lxxxiv.

cile themselves unpleasantly in the folds of your garments."[1]

Among the animals which are represented in the sacred Bharhut sculptures, there are no less than fourteen quadrupeds, six birds, one snake, one fish, one insect (the flesh fly), one crocodile, two tortoises, one lizard and one frog.

According to the Buddhist theory, man may be born again in the form of either animal, bird or reptile, or he may be born as a god or demon. "If he be born in hell he is not thereby debarred from seeking salvation; and even if he be born in heaven as a god, he must some time leave his happy estate and seek for the condition of the perfect man who has attained Nirvāṇa, and is soon to achieve the only consummation for which it is worth while to live—extinction of personal existence in Pari-nirvāṇa."[2]

[1] Williams, p. 524. [2] Ibid, B., p. 122.

CHAPTER VI.

THE TEACHINGS OF BUDDHISM, CONCLUDED.

METAPHYSICS — THE SOUL — ATHEISM — POLYTHEISM — IDOLATRY — PRAYER — PESSIMISM — HEAVEN — HELL — SALVATION — MORALITY — NIRVĀṆA — PARI-NIRVĀṆA.

THE philosophical doctrines which were taught by Buddha consisted largely of a system of negations. The metaphysics of Buddhism were freely taught in the Vagra*kk*ḥedikā, or the Diamond Cutter,[1] which is not only an early work, but is one of the most widely read and highly valued of the metaphysical treatises of Japan.

"Dharma," says F. Max Müller, "in ordinary Buddhist phraseology, may be correctly rendered by 'law.' But in our treatise, dharma is generally used in a different sense. It means form (Greek, *eidos*), and likewise what is possessed of form, what is individual, in fact, what we mean by a thing or an object.

"What our treatise wishes to teach is that all objects, differing from one another, by their dharmas,

[1] This work was written originally in Sanskrit, and has been translated into Chinese, Tibetan, Mongol and Mandshu. The first Chinese translation is ascribed to Kumaragiva of the latter Tsin dynasty (A. D. 384-417), and an English translation of this was published by the Rev. S. Beal in the Journal of the Royal Asiatic Society in 1864-5.

are illusive, or, as we should say, phenomenal and subjective—that they are, in fact, of our own making, the products of our own mind. . . . And, hence, the Buddhist metaphysician tells us that things are but names, and being names they are neither what they seem to be, nor what they do not seem to be. There are, in fact, no objects independent of us; hence, whoever speaks of things or persons uses names only.

"We may speak of a dog, but there is no such thing as a dog. It is always either a greyhound or a spaniel, this or that dog, but dog is only an abstraction, a name, a concept of our mind. The same applies to quadruped, animal and being; they are all names, with nothing corresponding to them. *This is what is meant by the highest perfect knowledge, in which nothing, not even the smallest thing is known, or known to be known.* In that knowledge there is no difference; it is always the same, and, therefore, perfect. He who has attained this knowledge believes neither in the idea, that is, the name of a thing, nor the idea of a no-thing, and Buddha by using this expression, the idea or name of a thing, implies thereby that it is not the idea of a thing. This metaphysical agnosticism is represented as familiar even to children and ignorant persons, and if it were meant to be so the endless repetition of the same process of reasoning may find its explanation."[1]

It was clearly stated at the Congress of Religions[2]

[1] Sa. Bks. E. Vol. XLIX, p. xiv, Int. to the Vagrakkhedika.
[2] Congress of Religions held in Chicago, September, 1893.

that this extreme scepticism is really the popular view of the present followers of the Mahā-yāna Buddhism. A deputy sent by the leading sects in Japan submitted to the Congress an outline of the doctrines of the Mahā-yāna Buddhists, which had been carefully examined and approved by scholars belonging to six of the Buddhists sects in Japan; it was, therefore, published with authority, and in this document the doctrine was emphatically taught.

THE SOUL.

It is in harmony with this system of negation that Buddhism was constructed independently of the theory of a soul. The belief in a soul is represented as one of the primary delusions which must be abandoned at the very first stage of the Buddhist path. Man is never the same for two consecutive moments, and there is within him no abiding principle whatever.

In the Sabbāsava Sutta, in speaking of the brethren who "consider unwisely," Buddha says: "As something true and real he gets the notion: 'I have a self' . . . as something true and real he gets the notion: 'By myself, I am conscious of myself.' . . . Or, again, he gets the notion: 'This soul of mine can be perceived, it has experienced the result of good and evil actions committed here and there; now, this soul of mine is permanent, lasting, eternal, and has the quality of never changing, and will continue forever and ever!'

"This, brethren, is called the walking in delusion, the puppet show of delusion, the writhing of delusion, the fetter of delusion. Bound, brethren, with this fetter of delusion, the ignorant, unconverted man becomes not free from birth, decay and death; from sorrows, lamentation, pains, griefs, and from expedients (the practice of rites and ceremonies and the worship of gods)—he does not become, I say, free from pain."[1]

No true Buddhist, therefore, believes in the passing of a soul from one body to another, but rather in the passing on of the merit or demerit resulting from one's actions. It is this act force (karma) combined with upadana (clinging to existence) which is the connecting link between each man's past, present and future bodies. Buddhists appear to be entirely unconscious of the inconsistency involved by claiming that personality is transmitted when there is no consciousness of any identity. Neither do they seem aware that there is any incongruity in claiming that Buddha could remember the experience of all his past lives, even though there was no conscious entity which survived the death of either body.

ATHEISM.

It is entirely in harmony with this system of negations that Buddha claimed that there was no god higher than himself. "Buddhism has no creator, no creation, no original germ of all things, no soul of the world, no personal, no impersonal, no supermundane, no antemundane principle."[2] The idea of a personal creator is not only denied, but Buddha claimed to find no one in the universe who was his own equal.

[1] Sabbasava Sutta, 10-12. [2] Williams, B., 117.

An ascetic by the name of Upāsaka came to him to inquire of whom he had learned his philosophy, whereupon Buddha replied as follows: "I have no teacher; there is no one who resembles me. In the world of gods I have no equal. I am the most noble being in the world, the irrefutable teacher, the sole all-pervading Buddha."

In one section of the Vinaya Piṭaka a story is told of a Brāhman who ventured to inquire why it was that Buddha did not honor the aged Brāhmans by rising in their presence and inviting them to be seated. Buddha replied: "Brāhman, I do not see any one in the heavenly worlds, nor in that of Māra, nor among the inhabitants of the Brahmā worlds, nor among gods or men, whom it would be proper for me to honor, or in whose presence I ought to rise up, or whom I ought to request to be seated. Should the Tathāgata (Buddha) thus act toward any one, that person's head would immediately fall off."[1]

But, although he did not acknowledge any being in the universe to be superior to himself, he did recognize the various gods of the Hindū pantheon, and it will be remembered that it was claimed he was born forty-three times as a tree god. "These gods or spirits were preserved very much in the previous order of precedence, and were all (except Māra, the Evil One, and his personal following) supposed to be passably good Buddhists. They were not feared, but patronized as a sort of fairies, usually beneficent, though always more or less foolish and ignorant.

[1] Quoted by Max Müller, Science of Rel., p. 171.

They were no longer worshiped, for they were considered less worthy of reverence than any good and wise man. They were not eternal—all of them, even the highest, being liable to death. If they behaved well, they were reborn under happy outward conditions, and might even look forward to being born sometime as men. No exception was made in the case of Brahmā. He also was evanescent, was bound by the chain of existence, the result of ignorance, and could only find salvation by walking along the eightfold path. It must be remembered that the Brahmā of modern times—the God of the ardent theism of some of the best of the later Hindūs—had not then come into existence; that conception was one effect of the influence of Mohammedan and Christian thought upon Hindū minds. But even if the idea of Brahmā were all the same as the idea of a god, a union with him would mean merely a temporary life as an angel in the Brahmā heavens."[1]

The radical atheism of Buddha, concerning the existence of any superior being, resulted in absurd polytheism among his followers.

POLYTHEISM.

He taught that man has no Father to whom he can appeal for aid or sympathy, but the higher sentiments of the human heart naturally reach upward, seeking some object of veneration, and no man can set his affections upon a blank or an abstraction. Hence there are now multitudes of gods in the Buddhist pantheon.

[1] Sa. Bks. E., Vol. XI, p. 163-164.

We have the first or lowest class of Brahmā gods inhabiting the lowest tiers of their abodes, the second class inhabiting the second tier, and the third class inhabiting the highest of the three tiers. But there are many other classes of gods besides those belonging to the Brahmā abodes. Indra was the most popular deity of the early Buddhists, and the Dhamma-pada mentions also Agni, the god of fire, and again Antaka, god of death, sometimes identified with Māra or Yama, "ruler in hell." The Buddhism of the North became identified with Śaivism, Śāktism, Magic, and even with Tāntrism[1] with its horribly loathsome accompaniments.

In the northern countries, various forms of Śiva and of his wife are honored, and their images are found in the temples. Sometimes bloody sacrifices are offered to them. Among the female deities the various forms of Tārā[2] are chiefly worshiped and regarded as Śaktis of the Buddhas. It is held by the disciples of the more advanced Mahā-yāna, especially in Nepāl, that there are five Śaktis or female energies (corresponding to five human Buddhas), but the goddess Tārā was also worshiped by Buddhists in India proper.

Among the many shrines at Ceylon there are some which are dedicated to a demonical goddess called Paṭṭini,[3] and every disease, every calamity, has its presiding demon, and all such demons are the servants of Buddha. Among other supernatural beings of Hindū

[1] The worship of the female principle (Sakti).

[2] The images of Tara (the wife or Sakti of one of the Buddhas) represent her as a green sedent figure, with her right hand on her knee and her left holding a lotus.

[3] A standing image of the goddess Pattini may be seen in the British Museum.

mythology that were adopted with slight changes by the Buddhists, we find the Pretas. These are supposed to partake of the nature of ghosts and goblins who have at one time inhabited the earth, and they are represented as being of gigantic size and terrific appearance; they are constantly suffering with hunger and thirst, yet never able to eat or drink on account of their contracted throats. They are sometimes represented as trying to eat dead bodies or their own flesh.

The Asuras are evil demons who, like the Titans of Greek mythology, are always at war with the gods. Closely connected with them are the Rākshasas, with their strongly developed man-eating propensities. There are also very malignant demons, called Piśāćas, who are the authors of all evils.

An important feature is also found in the Nāgas, and to these constant allusion is made. They properly belong to a class of serpent demons, having human faces and serpent-like lower extremities.

They are introduced into Buddhist sculptures as worshipers of Buddha and friends of all Buddhists. The Nāga Mućalinda who sheltered Buddha was a real serpent. The Nāga-kanyās or female Nāgas (serpents from the waist downward) are frequently mentioned.[1]

There are, too, the Mahoragas or great dragons, who also belong to the serpent class of demons, and there are many other classes which it would be too tedious to enumerate.

[1] An interesting image of a Naga-kanya may be found in the Museum of the Indian Institute at Oxford University It belongs to a collection of Buddhist antiquities, which was kindly loaned by Mr. R. Sewall, of the Madras Civil Service.

The worship of devils and demons existed in Ceylon before the introduction of Buddhism, but it was readily adopted by the new system, and the hideous rites connected therewith became a prominent feature.

IDOLATRY.

The pandits claim there was no idolatry in India until the Buddhists set the example of worshiping material objects and images, and, although it seems probable that material impersonations of the forces of nature existed before Buddha's time, there is no evidence of actual idolatry at the time the Ṛig-veda was composed.

But during the reign of Buddhism, the development of every phase of idolatrous superstition reached a point of extravagance unparalleled in any other system in the world. The monks of Buddhism vied with each other in the fraud with which they constructed their idols. They manipulated them so that they seemed to give out light or to flash glances from their crystal eyes; made them deliver oracular utterances, or furnished them with movable limbs, so that a head would unexpectedly nod or a hand be raised to bless the worshiper.

Besides the countless images of Gautama Buddha, there are images of the Buddhas who preceded him, and Fa-hien records that he saw in Northern India a wooden image of Maitreya Bodhisat, eighty cubits in height, which on certain days emitted a brilliant light. Offerings were continually made to it by the kings in the surrounding countries.[1]

[1] Legge, 23.

It was not until the introduction of the worship of Avalokiteśvara that the followers of Buddha thought of endowing the figures of their deified saints with an extra number of heads and arms. This deity was represented with eleven heads, and these were generally arranged in four rows, each series of faces having a different complexion.[1]

In China this god is represented as a woman, with a thousand arms and a thousand eyes. She has her principal seat on the island of Poo-too, on the coast of China, which is a place of pilgrimage. There are two images of her in the British Museum, one with sixteen arms and the other with eight. Idols are far more numerous in Buddhist countries than among any other idolatrous people, and not only this, but there are many other sacred objects which Buddhists of all schools hold in veneration, such as relics, footprints, trees, utensils, bells, symbols and animals. In many instances homage is actually offered to these things. Tradition claims that Gautama once directed Ānanda to break off the branch of the pīpal tree under which he attained to Buddhahood, and plant it in the garden. "He who worships it," said Gautama, "will receive the same reward as if he worshiped me."[2] Whether or not there be any truth in this legend, we certainly have the best of authority from many sources that the Bodhi tree (or pīpal) is the most sacred of all the trees of Buddhism, and for centuries actual homage has been paid to it in Buddhist countries.

[1] The three faces resting on the neck are white, the three above yellow, the next three are red, the tenth head is blue, and the eleventh, that is, the head of his father, at the top of all, is red.—*Williams, p. 487.*

[2] Ibid, p. 517.

PRAYER.

As Buddha believed in no god except those Hindū deities who were considered inferior to himself, he of course taught his followers to utter no prayer in the true sense of the word. They could not make an appeal to a power in whose existence they did not believe. He established no real church; instead of a priesthood or clergy, ordained for the purpose of aiding men in their progress toward a glorious immortality, he founded an Order of Monks pledged to denounce human life as not worth living, and bound to abstain from all participation in human affairs. It is evident that there could be no place for genuine prayer in such a system of negations, therefore the three-refuge formula[1] was the only substitute of the early Buddhists, and in Ceylon it is maintained to this day that this is the only form of prayer that should ever be used. Other formulas, however, came into use, and it is supposed that merit may be accumulated by the constant repetition of them. The most common form used in Tibet consists of the sentence: "Om! maṇi, padme Hūm." (Om! the jewel in the lotus.)[2] This is called the Maṇi, or Jewel prayer, and the Tibetan believes it to be a panacea for all evil, the treasury of all knowledge and the summary of all religion. The oftener it is repeated the shorter will be

[1] See p. 134.

[2] It is thought that an occult meaning underlies the jewel lotus formula, and that many who repeat it are ignorantly doing homage to the self-generative power supposed to inhere in the universe—a power pointed at by the popular Sankhya theory of the union of Prakriti and Purusha, and by the universal worship of the Linga and Yoni throughout India. (See Williams, B., p. 372; also Koeppen's note, Brahmanism and Hinduism, p. 33.)

the individual's course through the six forms of existence. Although not repeated like a prayer, in the sense of a petition, the words are murmured everywhere, and also written upon rolls of paper and inscribed in cylinders,[1] every revolution of which is supposed to repeat the mystic sentence. These revolutions are credited as so much "prayer merit," and a metallic cylinder, containing the words, is carried in the hand and whirled around like a child's toy. The revolutions must always be in a particular direction (with the sun), for, if by chance it revolved the other way, its rotations would be set down to the debtor rather than the creditor side of the owner's account.

It is said that when Baron Schilling visited a certain convent he found the Lāmas occupied in preparing one hundred millions of copies of "Om! maṇi, padme Hūm," to be inserted in a prayer cylinder. He also states that the inscription relating to the foundation of the monastery of Hemis records the setting up of three hundred thousand prayer cylinders along the walls and passages of the monastery.[2]

Although this is especially true of Northern Buddhism, still the prayer wheel is also common in Japan, where civilization has obtained so strong a hold, and other methods are often used. An eye witness gives the following description of an idol seen in Japan: "In one shrine is a large idol spotted all over with pellets of paper, and hundreds of these may be seen

[1] A complete temple of Buddha, with praying machines, bells, sacred towels, idols, etc., has recently been brought from the Orient to Philadelphia.

[2] Dr. Schlagintweit, p. 121.

sticking to the wire netting which protects him. A worshiper writes his petition on paper, or, better still, has it written by a priest, chews it to a pulp and spits it at the divinity. If, having been well aimed, it passes through the wire and sticks, it is a good omen, but if it lodges in the netting the prayer has probably been unheard. On the left there is a shrine with a screen to which innumerable prayers have been tied. On the right sits one of Buddha's original disciples. A Koolie with a swelled knee applied it to the knee of the idol, while one with inflamed eyelids rubbed his eyelids upon it."[1]

BELLS.

A very important part of a monk's equipment in Tibet is the prayer bell which is rung to accompany the repetition of prayers. The object of ringing bells during worship is to call the attention of the beings who are worshiped, or to keep off evil spirits by combining the noise with the waving of the handle. In Burma bells abound everywhere. They are never rung in peals or with a clapper; they are used to draw the attention of the deities and spirits to the act of worship, and thus secure the proper registration of the prayer merit. When a man has finished his repetitions he strikes the bell with a piece of wood or other sacred implement, and the more noise he makes the more effective it is supposed to be in calling attention to his meritorious act.

"Having thus begun," says Renan, "with pure

[1] Bird, "Unbeaten Tracks in Japan." (Murray, London.)

negation, Buddhism must drift into the most unrestrained superstition. The needs of the human heart resumed the ascendant; the influence of Śaivaism gave access to all mythological complications. . . . At the same time moral character disappears; religion consists only in turning the wheel, making statuettes of Buddha and offering flowers to the statuettes. Pious Buddhists spend their time in counting the revolutions of the wheel, calculating chimerical numbers, and beating drums to drive away the demons. All is pure idolatry."[1]

Perhaps the great French critic is somewhat severe, for, although their prayers may be repeated by machinery, written upon paper or inscribed on rocks, still there is probably something of the spirit of devotion connected even with idolatry and superstition.

PESSIMISM.

Buddha was the prince of pessimists, and in describing the misery of life he nowhere alludes to the happiness which may be derived from health, friends, love, or existence in a world of beauty. But he claims that his followers must believe his doctrine—must abandon wife and children—live upon alms as does the monk, suppress the individual self, and keep in mind the impermanence and impurities of the body. His "way of knowledge" was a knowledge of the idea that life was merely one link in a chain of existences, all of which were inseparably bound up in suffering and misery.

[1] Renan, Studies in Rel. Hist., p. 110.

The common doctrine that everything was for the worst, was freely taught by Brāhmanism, and continued to be a doctrine of Hindūism long after the disappearance of Buddhism. The great effort, therefore, was to find a way for deliverance from the misery believed to result from ceaseless rebirth, as the various schools were in harmony with each other in relation to the following sentiment:

"Enjoyments are alloyed by fear of sickness,
High rank may have a fall, abundant wealth
Is subject to exactions, dignity
Encounters risk of insult, strength is ever
In danger of enfeeblement by foes,
A handsome form is jeoparded by women,
Scripture is open to assaults of critics,
Merit incurs the spite of wicked men,
The body lives in constant dread of death—
One course alone is proof against alarms,
Renounce the world and safety may be won."[1]

HEAVEN.

Although heaven is only a temporary abode, still the founder of Buddhism believed in the old Hindū gods, and, while claiming that they were inferior to men, he promised his followers that they should be born after death in the heavens of the gods. According to the later Buddhistic theory, there were twenty-six successive tiers of heavens, one rising above the other.

In the center of the world system, on the upper

[1] Vairagya-sataka, III, p. 32, 50.

portion of the great mythical mountain Meru, we have the lowest heaven of the gods. This is above the worlds of ghosts, of demons and of men, also above the eight principal hells, and here abide the four great champions who guard the earth and heavens from the demons who are constantly assailing them from below.

The second is the heaven of Indra, who was the favorite god of the Hindūs for centuries.

The third heavens are inhabited by beings called Yāmas. They take no part in the strife which is constantly waged by the gods of the two lower heavens against the demons, and who are unable to advance into these higher regions.

The fourth heaven is that of the Tushitas or perfectly contented beings. This is a peculiarly sacred region, and is the home of those who are destined to become Buddhas.

The fifth region of happiness is inhabited by beings who constantly enjoy themselves with pleasures provided by themselves.

The sixth heaven is the abode of beings called Māras, and are "lords of sensuous desires." They are ruled over by a chief Māra who tempts men, and is always on the watch to enter the citadel of the body by way of the eye or the ear. He is sometimes represented as the Buddhist Satan, and sometimes as a superior god. One of his names is Kāma (desire).

Above these, there are sixteen other and higher heavens, which are occupied by different classes, and high above these are worlds which are inhabited by formless entities. In the first of these "formless worlds" are beings who are capable of conceiving the idea of infinite space. In the second are those who can conceive of infinite intelligence. In the third are those who can conceive the idea of absolute nonentity, or the doctrine that nothing whatever exists anywhere. The fourth of these, and highest of all the twenty-six, is occupied by "beings who abide in neither consciousness or unconsciousness, and this is considered the most sublime of all conditions in the heavenly world, and belongs to mystical Buddhism."[1]

HELL.

The descriptions of hell are very graphic, and the doctrine of the Buddhist contains no forgiveness. "Not in the heavens," says the Dhamma-pada, "not in the midst of the sea . . . wilt thou find a place where thou canst escape the force resulting from thy evil action."[2] In Brāhmanism, also, the influence of his own karma or action is universal in determining the form of every being at the time of his rebirth.

A passage in the Deva-duta-sutta represents king Yāma as pronouncing the doom of a wicked man thus: "These, thy evil deeds, are not the work of others; thou alone hast done them all; thou alone must bear the fruit. And then the warders of hell drag him to a place of torment, rivet him to red-hot iron, plunge him into glowing seas of blood, torture him on heaps of burning coal; and he dies not until the last residue of his guilt has been expiated."[3]

1 Williams, B., p. 213.
2 Dhamma-pada, 127.
3 Translated by Oldenberg.

Although the punishment of hell is not eternal, its shortest duration is five hundred of the years of hell, each day of which equals fifty years of earth.[1]

In Brāhmanism there are twenty-one hells, while Buddhism had originally only eight; later, however, there came to be one hundred and thirty-six divisions for the reception of different offenders. These hells are all in tiers one above the other, and they lie deep under the earth in the lower regions of the Ćakra-vala.

One of the most important temples at Ceylon is the temple of "the sacred eye tooth," and its walls are decorated with colored frescoes of the eight principal hells. Some of those who are undergoing purgatorial torments are represented as being cut in pieces by demons, or fixed on red-hot iron spikes; others are torn asunder with glowing tongs, or they are being sawn in two with saws; others are being crushed between rocks or consumed by flames entering the different apertures of their bodies.[2]

The Burmese authorities thus describe the hell to which Deva-datta was condemned for repeatedly attempting the life of Buddha: "His feet are sunk ankle deep in burning marl. His head is incased with a red-hot iron metal cap down to the lobe of the ears. Two large red-hot iron bars transfix him from the back to the front, two horizontally from right to left, and one impales him from head to foot."[3]

The following description of a portion of the punishments which are experienced in the various hells of Buddhism is given in the Buddha-*k*arita: "These

[1] Williams, 115–122. [2] Ibid, 454. [3] Shway Yoe's "Burman," I, 122.

living beings under the influence of evil actions pass into wretched worlds . . . and, being born in a dreadful hell, full of terrors, are miserably tortured, alas! by many kinds of suffering. Some are made to drink molten iron of the color of fire; others are lifted aloft screaming on a red-hot iron pillar; others are baked like flour, thrown with their heads downward into iron jars; others are miserably burned in heaps of heated charcoal; some are devoured by fierce, dreadful dogs, with iron teeth; others by gloating crows, with iron beaks, and all made, as it were, of iron; some, wearied of being burned, long for cool shade; these enter like bound captives into a dark-blue wood, with swords for leaves; others, having many arms, are split like timber with axes, but even in that agony they do not die, being supported in their vital powers by their previous actions."[1]

An earlier authority than the one above quoted is the Mahā-vagga, which is considered one of the most ancient of the Pāli works. It is here that we find Buddha's own description of the punishment of backbiters:

"To the place where one is struck with iron rods, to the iron stake with sharp edges he goes; then there is for him food as appropriate, resembling a red-hot ball of iron.

"For those who have anything to say there, do not say fine things, they do not approach with pleasing

[1] This doctrine in regard to the punishment of the wicked is given as a part of the enlightenment which Buddha attained under the Bo-tree, and this was the "true knowledge" which was gained in the second watch. (See Buddha-karita, Bk. XIV, 10–16.)

faces; they do not find refuge from their sufferings, they lie on spread embers, they enter the blazing pyre.

"Covering them with a net, they kill them there with iron hammers; they go to dense darkness, for that is spread out like the body of the earth.

"Then they enter an iron pot, they enter a blazing pyre, for they are boiled in those iron pots for a long time, jumping up and down in the pyre.

"Then he who commits sin is surely boiled in a mixture of matter and blood; whatever quarter he inhabits he becomes rotten there from coming in contact with matter and blood.

"Again they enter the sharp Asipattavana with mangled limbs; having seized the tongue with a hook the different watchmen of hell kill them.

"Then they enter Vetaraṇī that is difficult to cross, and has got streams of razors with sharp edges; there the fools fall in, the evil-doers after having done evil.

"There black mottled ravens eat them who are weeping, and dogs, jackals, great vultures, falcons and crows tear them."[1]

The reader can but note that he who could invent such tortures as these to be visited upon his fellow-creatures does not spare the life of the serpent or the insect from a feeling of genuine humanity, but rather on account of his belief in metempsychosis. It is difficult for either a Hindū or a Buddhist to draw a line of demarkation between gods, men and animals when the same living being may exist as a god, or a man or an animal.

[1] Maha-vagga, Kokaliya-sutta, 11-19.

SALVATION.

The true Buddhist does not "seek for glory, honor and immortality;" on the contrary, his every effort is to avoid a future life. The whole system being founded upon the declaration that "all life, even in heaven, is misery," the great desideratum is the final escape from the endless wheel of existence.

"Of deliverance of that from which we are to be delivered," says Oldenberg, "of the way in which we shall be delivered of this, and nothing else . . . do the sermons of Buddha, as rule, treat. God and the universe trouble not the Buddhist; he only knows one question: 'How shall I, in this world of suffering, be delivered from suffering?'"[1]

His "way of knowledge" was a knowledge of the truth that all life was misery, and the two causes of suffering were lust and ignorance. The first cure was the suppression of lust and desire, especially for all desire for continued existence. The second cure was the removal of ignorance—ignorance of the fact that all life is misery—that the misery of life is caused by indulging in lusts, and will cease by suppressing them.

But, although he claimed that all life proceeded from ignorance, he nevertheless taught that life in one of the heavens was better than life in one of the hells, and neither a higher form of life nor the great aim of Nirvāṇa could be attained without right action, meditation and true knowledge.

[1] Oldenberg, B., p. 130.

MORALITY.

Buddhism, like Manu, made morality the basis of law; it stimulated good conduct by its doctrine of repeated births, and by the pictures of a multitude of heavens, while it deterred its followers, as far as possible, from evil conduct by its vivid pictures of terrible hells. It could not speak of sin as an offense against God, as it recognized no deity higher than man; it, therefore, spoke of "demerit," and promised to those who attained perfection that they should be "free from pain."

The moral code soon passed beyond the system which Buddha presented in his "eight-fold path," but Dr. Oldenberg has shown that we may still trace out the leading duties of external life and internal mental concentration. The five fundamental prohibitions were formulated at an early day; indeed, some of them were taught by the Jewish law-giver centuries before the birth of Buddha:

1. Thou shalt not kill.
2. Thou shalt not steal.
3. Thou shalt not commit adultery.
4. Thou shalt not lie or bear false witness.
5. Thou shalt not drink strong drink.

Besides these, five other commandments were given, and these were for the benefit of the monks:

6. Eat no food except at stated times.
7. Use no wreaths, ornaments or perfumes.
8. Use no high or broad bed, but only a mat on the ground.

9. Abstain from dancing, singing, music and worldly spectacles.

10. Own no gold or silver of any kind, and accept none.

All gambling and games of chance were prohibited, and sometimes five renunciations are named: The renunciation of wife, of children, of money, of life, and of craving for existence in future births.

There are also six (now ten) transcendent virtues, called Paramitas.

NIRVĀṆA.

This term was not original with Buddha; it was current in Gautama's time, and certainly occurs in the Mahā-bhārata, some portions of which are of great antiquity. It is now common, however, to both Brāhmanism and Buddhism. The subject has caused much discussion among scholars, and the principal cause of the difficulty is the contradictory teaching of the native authorities upon the question.

The meaning of the word is "extinction," "blown out," or "the state of a blown-out flame." The Buddhist who arrives at perfection is supposed to be "blown out" (if we may use Buddhist phraseology) like a lamp. Some Orientalists, however, claim that the word means merely the extinction of all passions and desires, and the attainment of a condition which is free from all pain, all thought, all action and all feeling—a condition which is "neither consciousness nor unconsciousness," while others argue that it represents complete and final extinction. The discussions upon this subject are not by any means of modern origin, for the different schools of Buddhists in India, and even the philosophers of the same school, propounded many opinions as the explanation of this term, and the teachers maintained various theories upon the question.

But we cannot expect that Nirvāṇa should always be explained in the same way by a system which is so elastic that it changes its front to suit the characteristics or opinions of every country which it approaches. Buddha himself frequently spoke of his approaching death as the "final extinction of the Tathāgata" (or Buddha). He also spoke repeatedly of "passing away by that utter passing away in which nothing whatever remains behind."[1]

And again: "The body of the Perfect One, O disciples, subsists cut off from the stream of becoming. As long as his body subsists, so long will gods and men see him; if his body be dissolved, his life run out, gods and men shall no more behold him."[2]

On the death of one of his disciples he gave utterance to the following sentiment: "Dissolved is the body, extinct is perception; the sensations have all vanished away. The confirmations have found their repose; the consciousness has sunk to its rest."[3]

When the venerable Godhika had passed away, it is said that the followers of Buddha saw a cloud of smoke moving around the corpse, and they asked the Teacher what it meant.

"That is Māra the Wicked One, O disciples," replied Buddha. "He is looking for the noble Godhika's

[1] See p. 77. [2] Brahmajala sutta. (See the close.)
[3] Udana (Phayre MS.) See also Oldenberg, p. 266.

consciousness: where has the noble Godhika's consciousness found its place? But the noble Godhika has entered into Nirvāṇa; his consciousness nowhere remains."[1]

In these extracts and some others, we have the doctrine of eternal oblivion unmistakably taught by Buddha himself, but, at other times and under other circumstances, he persistently declined to give any definite answer whatever to the anxious questions of his followers.[2]

It is also repeatedly taught in the sacred texts that "the Perfect One neither exists after death nor does he not exist."[3]

After a careful examination of the subject, Dr. Oldenberg says: "Does the path lead into a new existence? Does it lead into the Nothing? The Buddhist creed rests in delicate equipoise between the two. The longing of the heart that craves the eternal has not nothing, and yet the thought has not a something which it might firmly grasp. Farther off the eternal could not withdraw itself from belief than it has done here, where, on the point of merging into the Nothing, it threatens to evade the gaze."[4]

Professor Childers has attempted to reconcile the conflicting statements of the Buddhists on this subject by the following explanation: "It is well known that in the Buddhist books there are two distinct sets of epithets applied to Nirvāṇa, the one implying a state of purity, tranquillity and bliss, and the other imply-

[1] Samyutta Nikaya, Vol. I, fol. ghi. Ibid, 281. [2] Ibid, 277-283.
[3] Samyutta Nikaya, Vol. II, fol. no, seq. [4] Oldenberg, B., p. 284.

ing extinction and annihilation. This circumstance has given rise to endless discussions relative to the true nature of Nirvāṇa, the result being that most conflicting views have been held on this question by European scholars."

"The theory which I propose is one which, *if true*, will, I think, meet all difficulties and reconcile the expressions in the Buddhist texts, even the most opposite and antagonistic. It is: That the word Nirvāṇa is applied to *two different things;* first, to the annihilation of existence, which is the ultimate goal of Buddhism, and, secondly, to the state of sanctification, which is the stepping-stone to annihilation, and without which annihilation cannot be obtained."[1]

"Buddhism," says Max Müller, "if tested by its own canonical books cannot be freed from the charge of Nihilism. . . . The ineradicable feeling of dependence on something else, which is the mainspring of all religion, was completely numbed in the early Buddhist metaphysicians, and it was only after several generations had passed away, and after Buddhism had become the creed of millions, that this feeling returned with increased warmth, changing the very nothing into a paradise and defying the very Buddha who had denied the existence of a deity. . . . In India also, Buddhism, as soon as it became a popular religion, had to speak a more human language than that of metaphysical Pyrrhonism. But if it did so, it was because it was shamed into it. This we may see from the very nicknames which the

[1] Childers, Trübner's Literary Record, June 25, 1870.

Brāhmans applied to their opponents. They called them Nāstikas—those who maintain there is nothing."[1] "I pointed out," he says, "on a former occasion that if we derive our ideas of Nirvāṇa from the Abhidharma . . . we cannot escape the conclusion that it meant *perfect annihilation.* Nothing has been brought forward to invalidate Burnouf's statements on this subject; much has since been added, especially by Barthélemy Saint-Hilaire, to strengthen and support them. . . . No person, reading with attention the metaphysical speculations on Nirvāṇa contained in the Buddhist canon, can arrive at any other conviction than that expressed by Burnouf, viz.: that Nirvāṇa, the highest aim, the *summum bonum* of Buddhism, is the absolute nothing."[2] He calls attention, however, to the very apparent fact that, although Buddhism teaches it, it does not necessarily follow that it was the sentiment of Buddha himself, who repeatedly evaded the question, and still, at times, he taught most explicitly that there would be no consciousness of the perfected one after death.[3]

Rhys Davids claims (as does Childers) that while Nirvāṇa is not in itself absolute extinction, it nevertheless leads to the shoreless sea of oblivion. "When a Buddhist has become an Arahat," he says, "when he has reached Nirvāṇa, he has extinguished sin, but he is still alive; his body with all its powers (that is, the fruits of his former sins) still remains. These,

[1] Chips, Vol. I, pp. 280, 281.
[2] Max Müller, Science of Religion, p. 178.
[3] Chips, Vol. I, p. 230.

however, will soon pass away; there will then be nothing left to bring about a new individual, and the Arahat will be no longer alive or existent in any sense at all. He will have reached complete extinction."[1] The solution presented by Sir Monier Monier-Williams is much the same. He argues that Nirvāṇa is not in itself necessarily the annihilation of all existence—it is the absence of pain, and also of demerit,[2] and of all thought and all work. "It is not consciousness, neither is it unconsciousness."[3]

PARI-NIRVĀṆA.

Besides Nirvāṇa we have another term—Pari-nirvāṇa; that is, "without remains or remnants of the elements of existence."[4] This is the oblivion to which Rhys Davids refers when he says that "Death, utter death, with no new life to follow, is the *result* of Nirvāṇa."[5] It is the condition to which Childers refers when he says that "Nirvāṇa is the stepping stone to annihilation." It is what Williams calls "the extinction of personal existence in Pari-nirvāṇa."[6]

We see, therefore, that the efforts of scholars to reconcile the contradictory teaching of the Buddhist

[1] Rhys Davids, B., p. 113.

[2] As Buddhism had no God in its system, neither could it have any sin in our sense of the word. "By an unrighteous act it meant an act producing suffering and demerit of some kind, and it bade every man act righteously in order to escape suffering, and thus work out his own perfection—that is, his own self-extinction."—*Williams, B., p. 124.*

[3] Ibid, p. 141.

[4] Childers' Pali Dictionary.

[5] Rhys Davids, B., p. 114.

[6] Williams, B., p. 122.

authorities upon this subject are quite harmonious after all. There are shades of thought and definition, it is true, but they agree that the *summum bonum* of Buddhist ambition is the absolute nothing. The only question being whether Nirvāṇa itself is utter extinction or only a half conscious condition which is to be succeeded by eternal oblivion.

It is true that, in modern times, Buddhists who have intercourse with Christian countries sometimes claim that "Nirvāṇa means union and communion with God, the absorption of the individual soul by the Divine essence." But no position could be more absurd than this, in view of the fact that true Buddhism believes in no God with whom a union could be formed, and no soul to be absorbed if, indeed, it did recognize a Divine essence. "Buddha himself," says Max Müller, "was certainly an atheist; therefore, if Nirvāṇa was not (in his mind) complete annihilation, still less could it have been absorption into the Divine essence. It was nothing but selfishness — in the metaphysical sense of the word — a relapse into that being which is nothing but itself. This is the most charitable view which we can take of Nirvāṇa, even as conceived by Buddha himself, and it is the view which Burnouf derived from the canonical books of the Northern Buddhists."[1]

[1] Chips, Vol. I, p. 284.

CHAPTER VII.

THE BUDDHIST ORDER OF MONKS.

ORDINATION OF THE BHIKKHUS OR MONKS — RULES FOR THEIR DIRECTION — UNSANITARY LAWS — UNSANITARY CLOTHING — PROTECTION FROM VENOMOUS SERPENTS — THE SERPENT WHO JOINED THE ORDER — NUNS — BUDDHA'S PROPHECY — RESULTS OF MONKHOOD.

THE foundations of Buddhism were not laid upon the sacred hearthstone of pure family life; on the contrary, he admonished his followers to forsake their wives and children, abandon their homes and form themselves into an Order of Monks. This organization was not a hierarchy. It had no ecclesiastical organization; its first head, the Buddha, appointed no successor. It was not a church, and it had no rite of ordination in the true sense. It was a brotherhood, in which all were under certain obligations and restraints, and were pledged to the propagation of the doctrine that all life was misery, whether on earth or in heaven, and that life, whether in present or future bodies, could only be avoided by a long course of discipline. The founding of a monastic brotherhood of this kind, which made personal extinction its final aim, and which might be co-extensive with the world, was Buddha's chief aim.

This Order began with ten members, but its growth was rapid and, in many ways, phenomenal. It is true that the warfare which he waged against marriage excited the opposition of the people. They complained that the practical working of his theories destroyed family life, and must also bring destitution, as the monks were forbidden to work, obtaining their living by carrying from door to door a bowl in which they received scraps of food.

Lay-brothers and lay-sisters were therefore a necessity. Married householders who were working people were actually necessary for the support of the monks. The formula for the admission of these members was extremely simple, being merely the repetition of the following words:

"I go for refuge to the Buddha,
I go for refuge to the Law,
I go for refuge to the Order." [1]

It was understood that they should abstain from the five gross offenses which are prohibited in the first portion of the decalogue,[2] but the principal test of loyalty was their willingness to serve the monks. They could not be called Buddhists, however, in the truest sense, unless they entered the great army of mendicants.

ORDINATION OF THE BHIKKHUS OR MONKS.

Monks were received into the Order by successive forms and ceremonies. At first, of course, there was

[1] Maha-v., I, 7, 10. [2] See p. 125.

no one who could ordain them except Buddha, and it was sufficient for him to say: "Come, follow me." The first converts were monks only; later, however, the three-refuge formula, as given above, was used for both monks and laymen. After this, it was said of converts that they "obtained the spotless eye of truth," when they "obtained the knowledge that whosoever is subject to the condition of origination is subject also to the condition of cessation." This is everywhere repeated, and when they had fully mastered this idea the Blessed One said to them: "Come, O Bhikkhus! well taught is the doctrine; lead a holy life for the sake of the complete extinction of suffering."[1]

Still later the ceremony became much longer and more complicated. The candidates were catechised in reference to their health, sex, caste and financial position. Also in reference to age, name and condition of robe and alms-bowl. When the men to be ordained became disconcerted and could not answer these questions, Buddha appointed an instructor for them. When the candidate was sufficiently taught to enable him to answer them, he was told to adjust his upper robe, to raise his joined hands, and to ask for the ordination by a prescribed formula three times repeated. Then a monk formally announced that the candidate was free from disqualifications—that his alms-bowl and robes were in due state. After this he was received by vote. "Then," said Buddha, "let them measure the shadow; tell the newly ordained monk what season and what date it is—tell him the whole formula and the 'four resources.'"[2]

[1] Maha-v., 2, 3. [2] Maha-v., I, 76, 1.

THE FOUR RESOURCES.

"I prescribe, O Bhikkhus! that he who confers the upasampadā ordination upon a Bhikkhu, tell him the four resources.

"'The religious life has morsels of food, given in in alms, for its resource. Thus you must endeavor to live all your life.'

"'The religious life has the robe made of rags, taken from the dust-heap, for its resource. Thus you must endeavor to live all your life.'

"'The religious life has dwelling at the foot of a tree for its resource. Thus you must endeavor to live all your life.'

"'The religious life has decomposing urine for its medicine. Thus you must endeavor to live all your life.'"[1]

There were extra allowances sometimes given besides the "resources," as meals by invitation or food distributed by ticket, and also certain articles, such as oil and molasses.

At that time a certain youth came to the Bhikkhus and asked them to ordain him. The Bhikkhus told him the four resources before ordination, whereupon he refused to receive the rite. When the fact was told to Buddha, he answered as follows: "You ought not, O Bhikkhus, to tell the resources to the candidates before their ordination. He who does so is guilty of a dukkaṭa offense.[2] I prescribe, O Bhik-

[1] Ibid, I, 30, 4.

[2] A slight offense for which no penance was required except confession.

khus, that you tell the resources to the newly ordained Bhikkhus immediately after their upasampadā."[1]

RULES FOR THE DIRECTION OF THE MONKS.

The Pātimokkha is one of the oldest of all the Buddhist text-books. The name seems to have owed its origin to the ancient Indian custom of holding sacred two periods in each month—the times of the new and the full moon. The Saṅgha fraternity made use of the gatherings at these meetings for confession. It was at these periods that each monk confessed to the assembled Order the faults he had committed and received penance therefor. The directions found in the Pātimokkha include not only penalties for lying, stealing and other immoralities, but the most trivial affairs of life are given a great degree of importance. For instance, the whole of the second section is devoted to directions concerning the rugs of the monks, and the following rules are a sample of others: "Whatsoever Bhikkhu shall have a rug made of pure black wool or goat's hair—that is an offense involving forfeiture. In case a Bhikkhu is having a new rug made, two parts should be taken of black wool, the third part of white, and the fourth brown. When a Bhikkhu is having a new rug made, a piece which is a span's width, should be taken from around the old one. If he has one made without taking a span's width from all round the old one—that is an offense involving forfeiture. Whatsoever Bhikkhu shall get a goat's wool washed or dyed, or combed out by a

[1] Maha-v., 1,31, 3.

Bhikshuni (or nun) who is not related to him—that is an offense involving forfeiture."[1]

Many pages are devoted to the proper time for receiving robes, the way they should be made, the length of time they should be worn, and many other particulars. They should be made of rags from a dust heap or a cemetery, or if of new cloth it must be torn into rags and sewn together. "A Bhikkhu who receives a new robe must choose one of three modes of disfigurement—either making a part of it dark blue, or marking it with black mud, or making part of it black."[2] Many pages are also devoted to the rules in relation to the shoes or slippers.

In relation to women the rules were very strict, the monks not being allowed to touch a woman's hand or walk along the road with her (except under certain conditions), or to preach the Dhamma to her in more than five or six words, "without the presence of a man who had arrived at the years of discretion." The grossest breach of morality, however, was ranked with the offense of having a needle-case made of the wrong material—each one being a Pākittiya.[3] These offenses range in their gravity with the dukkaṭa, and require only simple confession.[4]

UNSANITARY LAWS.

It must be confessed that, in some respects, the law of Buddha was very far from being sanitary.

[1] Patimokkha, Sec. iii, 17.
[2] Ibid, Sec. vi, 58.
[3] Compare Aniyata Dhamma, 2, and Pakittiya Dhamma, 45 and 44, with 86.
[4] See Kulla-vagga, XI, 1, 10.

For instance, the following statement is made in the Mahā-vagga: "Now, at that time, a certain Bhikkhu had a disease not human. He went to a place where swine were slaughtered, and ate the raw flesh and drank the blood. Thereby his sickness was abated. They told this thing to the Blessed One, and he replied: 'I allow, O Bhikkhus, in the case of disease not human, the use of raw flesh and blood.'"[1]

"Now, at that time," again says the Maha-vagga, "a certain Bhikkhu had jaundice." On this occasion the Buddha prescribed as a medicine an article too revolting for description.[2]

Although the killing of any animal or insect was strictly forbidden, still there is frequent mention of the eating of flesh, and on one occasion it was charged that "Sīha has killed a great ox and has made a meal for Gautama; the Gautama knowingly eats of the meat of an animal killed for this very purpose, and has thus become virtually the author of that deed (of killing the animal)." The offense seemed to consist in eating animals when the monks knew that they had been killed purposely for them.

"Let no one, O Bhikkhus, knowingly eat meat of an animal killed for that purpose. . . . I prescribe, O Bhikkhus, that fish is pure to you, if you have not seen, if you have not heard, if you do not suspect, that it has been caught specially to be given you."[3]

"At that time the king's elephants died . . . when the Bhikkhus came and asked for alms they

[1] Maha-v., VI, 10, 2. [2] Ibid, VI, 14, 7. [3] Ibid, VI, 31, 13-14.

gave them elephant's flesh. The Bhikkhus ate that elephant's flesh. The people were annoyed and became angry. 'How can they eat elephant's flesh? Elephants are an attribute of royalty. If the king knew that, they would not be in favor.' They told this thing to the Blessed One. 'Let no one, O Bhikkhus, eat elephant's flesh; he who does so commits a dukkaṭa offense.'

At that time the king's horses died, and when the Bhikkhus asked for alms they gave them horse flesh. Then the people were annoyed . . . and asked: "How can they eat horse flesh? Horses are an attribute of royalty. If the king knew that, they would not be in favor." Then they told this thing to the Blessed One: "Let no one, O Bhikkhus, eat horse flesh. He who does so commits a dukkaṭa offense."[1]

It will be noted that in these cases there is no suggestion that it was not healthful or proper to eat the flesh of animals that had died a natural death, but the offense is placed upon the ground that the king would be displeased if he knew that they had eaten of animals which "are an attribute of royalty." It is further stated that they ate dog's flesh, and, again, that they ate serpent's flesh.

"And the serpent king went to the place where the Blessed One was . . . and said to him: 'There are, Lord, unbelieving serpents who are disinclined (to the faith), these might do harm to the Bhikkhus, even on trifling occasions. Pray, Lord, let not their reverences eat serpent's flesh.' In consequence of that

[1] Maha, VI, 23. 10.

the Blessed One thus addressed them: 'Let no one, O Bhikkhus, eat serpent's flesh. He who does so commits a dukkaṭa offense."[1]

"They ate lion's flesh, then the lions, attracted by the smell of lion's flesh, fell on them in the forest. . . . Let no one, O Bhikkhus, eat lion's flesh. The same thing is repeated in the case of a tiger, panther, bear and hyena. In each case they are admonished not to eat the food, not because it was an offense against the law, but because the animals, attracted by the smell of their kind, attacked the monks. There is also, in these sacred Pāli texts, a story of a monk who was sick, and wanted some broth when there was no meat to be had. Whereupon, a devoted lay woman cut off a portion of her own flesh, and had a broth made of it for the sick man.[2] In case of snake-bite, the monks were given "ashes, manure, urine and clay."

Again, when a certain monk had taken poison, Buddha prescribed a most loathsome decoction to be taken into the stomach.[3]

They were allowed the fat of bears, of fish, of alligators, of swine and other animals, provided it was received, mixed and cooked at the proper time. "If the fat be received, O Bhikkhus! at the wrong time, cooked at the wrong time, mixed at the wrong time, and then taken, the Bhikkhu is guilty of three dukkaṭa offenses."

UNSANITARY CLOTHING.

Not only did they at times use the flesh of animals which had died a natural death, and take the most

1 Maha, VI, 23, 13. 2 Maha-v., VI, 23, 3. 3 Ibid, VI, 14, 6.

disgusting compounds of filth for medicine, but they were allowed to go to cemeteries for their robes. The whole of section four, in the eighth Khandhaka, is devoted to the proper conduct of monks toward each other during their visits to the cemetery for that purpose. At that time a party of monks went into a cemetery to get robes, and the others did not wait for their return. Therefore, they refused to divide the robes with those who did not wait for them, but the Buddha ordered them to divide with them. At another time, two parties went to the cemetery, but only those who arrived first were fortunate enough to obtain robes, and they refused to divide with the less fortunate party. On this occasion Buddha's decision was as follows: "I prescribe, O Bhikkhus! that you are not obliged to give a part against your will to those who have gone to the cemetery later than yourselves."[1] Not only were they allowed unsanitary food and clothing, but they were forbidden to bathe at intervals of less than half a month, except on special occasions.

PROTECTION FROM VENOMOUS SERPENTS.

As a safeguard against the bite of the venomous serpents which infest India, Buddha instructed his monks to repeat a formula in which they declared their great love for the four breeds of royal serpents.

"Now at that time a certain Bhikkhu died of the bite of a snake. They told this matter to the Blessed One. 'Now, surely, that Bhikkhu, O Bhikkhus, had

[1] Ibid, VIII, 1, 2, 4; I, 5.

not let his love flow out over the four royal breeds of serpents! Had he done so he would not die of the bite of a snake. . . . I allow you, O Bhikkhus, to make use of a safeguard for yourselves, for your security and protection, by letting your love flow out over the four royal breeds of serpents. And thus, O Bhikkhus, are you to do so:

"I love (here follow the names of the four royal breeds of snakes).

"I love live things that have no feet; the bipeds, too, I love.

"I love four-footed creatures, and things with many feet.

"Let no footless thing do hurt to me, nor thing that has two feet. . . . Made is my safeguard, made is my defense. Let living things retreat whilst I revere the Blessed One, the Buddhas, seven, supreme."[1]

This early statement has been expanded also into Jātaka, in which all the verses which are here given, and some others, are used as a snake charm.[2] In another place they were allowed supports to their beds as a protection from snakes, but they were forbidden to have them more than eight inches high.[3]

THE SERPENT WHO JOINED THE ORDER.

"At that time there was a serpent who was aggrieved at and ashamed of having been born as a serpent. Now he thought: 'What am I to do in

[1] Kulla-vagga, v, 6, 1.

[2] Khandha-vatta Jataka, No. 203, in Prof. Fausböll's edition, Vol. II, pp. 144-148.

[3] Kulla-vagga, vi, 2, 5.

order to become released from being a serpent and quickly to obtain human nature. . . . If I could obtain pabba*gg*ā I should be released from being a serpent and quickly obtain human nature.'

"Then that serpent, in the shape of a youth, went to the Bhikkhus and asked them for the pabba*gg*ā ordination; the Bhikkhus conferred on him the pabba*gg*ā and upasampadā ordinations.

"At that time the serpent dwelt with a certain Bhikkhu who arose at dawn, and was walking up and down in the open air. When the Bhikkhu had left, the serpent thought he was safe from discovery, and fell asleep in his natural shape. The whole Vihāra was filled with the snake's body; his windings jutted out of the window. Then the Bhikkhu thought: 'I will go back to the Vihāra,' and opening the door he saw the whole Vihāra filled with the snake's body and the windings jutting out of the window. Then he was terrified and cried out, bringing his friends to the scene.

"Then the serpent awoke in the noise, and sat down upon a seat. The Bhikkhus asked him who he was, and he answered: 'I am a serpent, reverend sirs,' and told them the whole story, and they told it to the Blessed One. The Blessed One ordered the fraternity of Bhikkhus to assemble, and then said to the serpent: 'You serpents are not capable of spiritual growth in this doctrine and discipline. However, serpent, go and observe fast on the fourteenth, fifteenth and eighth day of each half month; thus will you be released from being a serpent and quickly obtain human nature.'

"Then the serpent shed tears, and made an outcry and went away. Then the Blessed One said to the Bhikkhus: 'Let an animal that has not received the upasampadā ordination not receive it; if it has received it, let it be expelled from the fraternity.'"[1]

NUNS.

Important Buddhistic authorities[2] agree that women were indebted to the good offices of Ānanda for the privilege of taking holy vows. Gautamī, who had faithfully nursed the Buddha after the death of his mother, besought him repeatedly to allow women to enter the order, but he constantly refused. Such was her devotion that she succeeded in gathering together five hundred women, who shaved their heads, put on bhikshuni's clothing and followed him into the Natika country, coming into his presence wearied, ragged and covered with dust.

Here the faithful Gautamī again presented her plea, but only to be refused as on other occasions. She, therefore, took her seat outside of the house and wept. It was there that Ānanda saw her, and kindly inquired the cause of her grief. Upon learning it he went immediately to Buddha and presented a plea in her behalf.

"Ānanda," replied Buddha, "ask not that women be admitted to the order; for if women enter, the rules of the order will not last long. . . . If a field of sugar cane is blighted, it is worthless, good for nothing; so will it be, Ānanda, if women enter the

[1] Maha-vagga, 1, 63, 1. [2] Kulla-vagga, X, 1, 3; also Vinaya-pitaka.

order, the rules of the order will not last long."[1] He also compared women to the five kinds of dangerous serpents, the angry, the spiteful, the hating, the ungrateful, and the venomous.[2] Nevertheless, in response to Ânanda's repeated pleadings he gave Gautamī permission to enter the order if she complied with the following rules:

1. She must thoroughly understand the nature of a bhikshuni (or nun).

2. A bhikshuni being near bhikshus (or monks) shall be taught twice a month.

3. A bhikshuni shall not pass the period of *was*[3] in a place where there are no bhikshus.

4. A bhikshuni during *was* shall be sufficiently separated from the bhikshus, so as not to hear them or fear proximity.

5. A bhikshuni by words reviving recollections shall not damage the morals of a bhikshu.

6. A bhikshuni shall not be wrathful, abusive, nor do anything sinful.

7. A bhikshuni shall confess her sins to a bhikshu every fortnight.

8. A bhikshuni, though she has been ordained a hundred years, shall always speak kindly to a bhikshu, even if he be recently ordained. She shall honor him, rise up before him, reverence him, and bow down to him.[4]

Gautamī accepted these conditions, and she and

[1] Vinaya-pitaka, f. 330*a*.

[2] Tibetan Dulva, X, f. 127*b*.

[3] The period called "*was*" is, in Ceylon, the finest part of the year. It includes the four rainy months from June to October.

[4] Dulva, f. 331. Also Kulla-v., 10, 1, 4.

others were permitted to take the vows. Afterward, however, Ānanda was bitterly reproached for his agency in the matter of having an order of nuns founded. Kāsyapa is represented as saying to him: "Ānanda, thou wast the Blessed One's close attendant . . . but if thou sayest that thou hast done no wrong to the congregation, how comes it that when the Blessed One said that women were as dangerous as snakes, and said it would be wrong to admit them to the order, thou didst ask that they might be allowed to enter it?"

"Bear with me awhile," replied Ānanda. "I thought of all that Gautamī had endured, and how it was she that had nursed the Blessed One when his mother died. I only asked that women who are relatives and friends might enter the order—surely that was no subject of shame."

BUDDHA'S PROPHECY.

Although he had given permission for women to take the vows in compliance with the constant entreaty of Ānanda and the woman to whom he was indebted for his continued existence after the death of his mother, still Buddha also censured Ānanda for his part in the matter, and it was upon this occasion that Buddha uttered the memorable prophecy that his doctrine would continue only five hundred years.

"If, Ānanda, women had not received permission to go out from the household life and enter the homeless state under the doctrine and discipline of the Tathāgata, then would the pure religion have lasted long, the good law would have stood fast for a thousand years. But since, Ānanda, women have now received that permission, the pure religion, Ānanda, will not now last so long, the good law will now stand fast for only five hundred years."[1]

RESULTS OF MONKHOOD.

It must be confessed that Buddha was a woman-hater as well as a hater of the marriage covenant, and his Order of Monks resulted to a great extent in moral disaster. In herding men together and depriving them of the society of womanhood for life, he did violence to every instinct of nature and invited the worst of crimes.

"Of course an immediate result was that, although according to Buddha's ordinance, any one who aimed at perfect sanctity was bound to live a celibate life, the rule against marriage was admitted to be inapplicable to the majority of human beings living in the world. The mass of people, in short, were necessarily offenders against the primary law of Buddhism. Though called lay-Buddhists, they were not 'wise men' in the Buddhist sense of the term. There is evidence that among certain monkish communities, in northern countries, the law against marriage was soon relaxed. It is well known that at the present day Lamaseries in Sikkim and Tibet swarm with the children of the monks, though called their nephews and nieces. And far worse than this, Buddhism ultimately allied itself with Tāntrism, or the worship of the female principle

[1] Kulla-vagga, X, 1. 6.

(śakti), and under its sanction encouraged the grossest violations of decency and the worst forms of profligacy."[1]

Scholars have called attention to the "collection of moral horrors existing in some parts of the Pārājika books — the disgusting detail of every conceivable form of revolting vice, supposed to be perpetrated or perpetrable by the monks."[2]

"It is, indeed," says Williams, "one of the strange phenomena of the present day that even educated people are apt to fall into raptures over the precepts of Buddhism, attracted by the bright gems which its admirers delight in culling out of its moral code, and in displaying ostentatiously, while keeping out of sight all its dark spots, all its trivialities and senseless repetitions; not to speak of all those evidences of deep corruption beneath a whited surface — all those significant precepts and prohibitions in its books of discipline, which, indeed, no Christian could soil his lips by uttering."[3]

[1] Williams, B., p. 152.
[2] Ibid, n. p. 543. Also Columbo, "Nineteenth Century," July, 1888.
[3] B., p. 451.

CHAPTER VIII.

EARLY BUDDHIST LITERATURE.

LITERARY ACTIVITY IN THE EAST — THE ART OF WRITING — EXTENT OF THE BUDDHIST SCRIPTURES — THE DATE OF THE CANON — THE TRI-PIṬAKA — THE VINAYA TEXTS—CARE OF THE BOWLS — TOOTH STICKS — THE WONDERS OF BUDDHA — GREAT EFFICACY OF RECITATION — INTEGRITY OF THE TEXT.

THERE was a period of great intellectual activity in the East about five hundred years before Christ. Within a few decades, before and after this date, we find many prominent teachers and also kings, who were the patrons of letters.

Persia had her Zoroaster, and under Darius a collection of texts in the Aryan language was made and promulgated throughout the empire. The Hebrews had their Daniel, whose influence was felt at the court of the king, who held him captive; and China had Confucius, who was the exponent of her laws. Greece had her Pythagoras and her Socrates, while, according to Mitford, no Grecian state had its laws put in writing until about the same period.

In India this period was marked by the formation of the Upanishads, which contain the doctrinal portion of the Vedas, and it also witnessed the reformation of

Buddha, who led the reaction against the tyranny of the Brāhmanic priesthood. Here were the beginnings of a literature radically different from the hymns of the Vedas, although Buddhism is largely indebted to the philosophy of the Brāhmans.

There is a sublimity in the early Vedic hymns which is lacking in most of the later productions, and the genuine eloquence which is sometimes found in the extravagant description of Buddhist writers too often degenerates into coarse or commonplace expressions. Still, there are beautiful thoughts, which are worthy of a place in any school of letters, and we find also many admonitions to purity of thought and life, which, although not original with Buddha, belong to the universal code of ethics.

Various portions of the early literature of Buddhism have been considered in the foregoing pages;[1] there should be, however, some classification of the books belonging to the sacred canon.

It will be remembered that no claim of inspiration is made for these writings. This would have been inconsistent with the whole tenor of the teaching of a man who recognized no God higher than himself. The fact that these maxims and traditions were taught for generations, by recital only, may account for the constant repetitions which everywhere meet the eye, and were, perhaps, introduced as aids to the memory.

THE ART OF WRITING.

Max Müller claims that the practice of writing "came in toward the latter part of the Sūtra period,"[2]

[1] See pp. 45, 77, 85, 104. [2] Sutra period, about 500 B.C.

while Oldenberg and Rhys Davids[1] argue that the art was unknown in India during the age of Buddha, and for a long time afterward. This statement is questioned by Williams[2] and others; still it is certain that for some time after writing was known, it was considered desecration to make use of it for the preservation of the sacred books.[3]

Although writing may not have been commonly practiced by the Hindūs at this time, still it had been known in India, for, during the reign of Ahasuerus, king of Persia (who has been identified as Xerxes I), the king sent a written proclamation to the Jews who were in his dominions, and also to "the deputies and rulers of the provinces which are from India unto Ethiopia." This imperial decree was written in various languages, so that every people, including the Jews and Hindūs, received it in their own language and according to the writing of their own province.[4]

The Buddhists claim that their scriptures were reduced to writing in the first century before Christ,[5] but much of their literature has been produced since then, and Fa Hian says that even in his time (about four hundred years after Christ), the various masters handed down the doctrines by word of mouth through the whole of Northern India, and had no written

[1] Sa. Bks. E. Vol. XI, p. xxii.

[2] "The art of writing was not common in India at this time, but it is difficult to accept the theory of those who claim that it had not been invented." —*Williams, B., p. 19.*

[3] "Those who sell the Vedas," says the Maha-bharata, "and even those who write them, shall go to hell."

[4] Esth. viii, 8–11.

[5] See note to p. 43.

copies of them.[1] It is well known that among the Semitic races the art of writing was understood for hundreds of years before it became common in India.[2]

EXTENT OF THE BUDDHIST SCRIPTURES.

It is claimed that the bulk of this literature has been largely overestimated. Rhys Davids has made so thorough an examination of the subject that he has even counted the words in a portion of the Sūtras, and based his conclusion upon a careful calculation of the whole. "The Buddhist scriptures," he says, "including all repetitions and all those books which contain extracts from the others, contain rather less than twice as many words as are found in our Bible, and a translation of them into English would be

[1] Fa Hian, Ch. 36, q. by Rhys Davids, B., p. 240.

[2] See the early Assyrian tablets and also those of Egypt. In the winter of 1887 a very remarkable discovery was made among the mounds of Tel-el-Amarna in Upper Egypt. It was here that clay tablets were found bearing inscriptions in the Babylonian language, and when deciphered and translated, they proved to be copies of letters and dispatches from the kings and governors of Babylonia and Assyria, of Syria, Mesopotamia and Eastern Capadocia, of Phœnicia and Palestine. These imperishable documents prove that all over the civilized East, *in the century before the Exodus*, active literary intercourse was carried on through the medium of a common language.

It is evident, therefore, that throughout Western Asia, schools and libraries must have existed, in which clay tablets inscribed with cuneiform characters were stored up, and where the language and syllabary of Babylonia were taught and learned.

Such a library must have existed in the Canaanite city of Kirjath-Sepher, or "Book Town" of Judges i, 12, and if its site can ever be recovered and excavated, we may expect to find there its collection of books, written upon the imperishable clay.

Many dispatches from Palestine, which have been assigned to about the fifteenth century before Christ, have been recovered, translated and published. (See "Records of the Past," edited by Prof. A. H. Sayce, Vol. II, pp. 58-63.) The authenticity of the cuneiform dispatches found at Tel-el-Amarna, in Egypt, has lately received an unexpected confirmation from tablets found at Tel-el-Hesy, probably the Biblical Lachish.

about four times as long. Such a literature is by no means unmanageable."[1]

"These repetitions are so numerous that without them the Buddhist Bible would probably be shorter than ours. Thus, the whole of the Dhamma-pada and the Sutta-nipāta are believed to have been taken from other books; and even in the Nikāyas whole paragraphs and chapters are repeated under different heads; the Subha-Sutta, for instance, contains almost the whole of the Samaṇa-phala Sutta and a great part of the Brahmājala Sutta."[2] The bulky Kanjur and Tanjur of the Tibetans has been sufficiently translated to establish the fact that the principal portion of the matter was a translation from the same Sanskṛit originals which had been discovered in Nepāl by Mr. Hodgson.

THE DATE OF THE CANON.

The Buddhist canon has only been traced back to the first century before Christ, when (as the Buddhists claim) it was reduced to writing in Ceylon under king Vaṭṭagāmani, but the books undoubtedly contain much older matter. The Buddhists suppose that the canon was settled at the first Council,[3] or soon after the death of Buddha, being then handed down by oral tradition until it was committed to writing.

[1] Rhys Davids, B., p. 19.

[2] Burnouf, Lotus, 448, 465, note 5.

[3] This assemblage can scarcely with any fitness be called a Council. Nor can the fact of its meeting together in any formal manner be established on any trustworthy historical basis. . . . There, in all likelihood, they (the monks who were gathered together) made the first step toward a methodical arrangement, but it is doubtful whether any systematic collections were composed.—*Williams, p. 55.*

But there are many difficulties here, and the chronological evidence is far from satisfactory.

"The evidence on which we have to rely," says F. Max Müller, "is such that we must not be surprised if those who are accustomed to test historical and chronological evidence in Greece and Rome decline to be convinced by it. As a general rule I quite agree that we cannot be too sceptical in assigning a date to ancient books. . . . We have the commentaries on the Pāli canon translated or composed by Buddha-ghosha, who confessedly consulted various manuscripts. This was in the beginning of the fifth century of the Christian era, and there is nothing improbable, though I would say no more, in supposing that some of the manuscripts consulted by Buddha-ghosha dated from the first century before Christ." [1]

THE TRI-PIṬAKA.

The sacred canon of the Buddhists is called the Tri-piṭaka, or the "Three Baskets," and these are composed of smaller works. The first basket, or Vinaya, contains all that has reference to morality. The second contains the Sūtras,[2] or the discourses of Buddha. The third includes works treating on a variety of subjects—philosophy, metaphysics, discipline and ethics.

THE VINAYA TEXTS, OR FIRST BASKET.

These texts compose the "first basket," and they are divided into three sets of rules:

[1] Int. Dhamma-pada, pp. 12-14.

[2] Sutras in Sanskrit; the Pali word is Sutta, and the words are, therefore, sometimes used interchangeably.

1st. The Khandhaka in two collections, called the Mahâ-vagga, or great section, and the *K*ulla-vagga, or minor section.

2d. The Vibhaṅga, or systematic arrangement, and explanation of the Pātimokkha, or release precepts. These are the rules for setting free, through penances, those who had offended against the order.

3d. The Parivāra-pāṭha, which is a comparatively modern summary of the other two divisions.

Extracts have already been freely given from important portions of the Law, and these early texts also devote hundreds of pages to the most trivial acts in the daily life of the monks. For instance, much space is devoted to the proper care of the bowls in which they begged their daily bread.

CARE OF THE BOWLS.

"Now at that time the Bhikkhus put away water in their bowls, and the bowls were split. They told this thing to the Blessed One. 'You are not, O Bhikkhus, to put away your bowls with water in them. Whosoever does so is guilty of a dukkaṭa offense. I enjoin upon you, O Bhikkhus, to dry your bowls in the sunshine before you put them away.'

"Now at that time the Bhikkhus dried their bowls in the sunshine with water in them; and the bowls became evil smelling. They told this thing to the Blessed One. 'You are not, O Bhikkhus, to dry your bowls in the sunshine with water in them. Whosoever does so is guilty of a dukkaṭa. I allow you, O Bhikkhus, to empty out the water, and then warm the bowls before you put them away.'

"Now at that time the Bhikkhus put their bowls away in a warm place, and the color of their bowls was spoilt. They told this thing to the Blessed One. 'You are not, O Bhikkhus, to put your bowls away in a warm place. Whosoever does so is guilty of a dukkaṭa. I allow you, O Bhikkhus, to dry your bowls in a warm place, and then put them away.

"Now at that time a number of bowls were left in the open air without supports, and the bowls were turned over by a whirlwind and broken. They told this thing to the Blessed One. 'I allow you, O Bhikkhus, the use of supports for your bowls when they are left out.'

"Now at that time the Bhikkhus put their bowls away at the edge of the sleeping benches in the verandahs, and the bowls fell down and were broken." When they told this to the Buddha he reproved them in the same formula as before.

"Now at that time the Bhikkhus hung up their bowls on pins in the walls or on hooks. The pins or hooks falling down the bowls were broken." In this case Buddha reproved them as before.

"Now at that time the Bhikkhus put their bowls down on a bed or a chair, and sitting down thoughtlessly the bowls were broken." And again they were reproved.

"Now at that time the Bhikkhus kept their bowls in their laps, and rising up thoughtlessly they upset them and the bowls were broken."[1] The same formula is repeated hundreds of times in relation to the most trivial matters.

[1] *Kulla-vagga*, V, 9, 3–10, 1.

TOOTH STICKS.

Again in the matter of tooth sticks, as well as other trifles, long instructions are given; for instance, the following:

"Now at that time the Bhikkhus did not use tooth sticks, and their mouths got a bad odor. They told this matter to the Blessed One. 'There are five disadvantages, O Bhikkhus, in not using tooth sticks; it is bad for the eyes[1]—the mouth becomes bad smelling—the passages by which the flavors of the food pass are not pure—bile and phlegm get into the food—and the food does not taste well. These are the five disadvantages in not using tooth sticks. I allow you, O Bhikkhus, tooth sticks.'

"Now at that time they used long sticks, and even struck people with them. They told this thing to the Blessed One. 'You are not, O Bhikkhus, to use long tooth sticks. Whosoever does so shall be guilty of a dukkaṭa. I allow you, O Bhikkhus, tooth sticks up to eight finger breadths in length. . . . '

"Now at that time a certain Bhikkhu when using too short a tooth stick got it stuck in his throat. They told this matter to the Blessed One. 'You are not, O Bhikkhus, to use too short a tooth stick. Whosoever does so shall be guilty of a dukkaṭa. I allow you, O Bhikkhus, tooth sticks of four finger breadths long at the least.'"[2]

[1] It appears that Buddha actually believed that the use of tooth picks was good for the eyes. (See note 1, *K*ulla-vagga, v, 31.)

[2] *K*ulla-vagga, V, 31, 1-2.

THE WONDERS OF BUDDHA.

These early Pāli texts also give many of the "wonders" which are said to have been performed by Buddha. It is said of him that at one time he asked Kassapa to allow him to spend the night in the room where the sacred fire was kept. But the host objected, saying there was a venomous serpent, or Nāga king, having great supernatural powers, which occupied the room. When Buddha persisted, however, Kassapa gave his consent. When the Blessed One entered the room the snake was annoyed, and sent forth a cloud of smoke.

Then the "chief of men"[1] sent forth a cloud of smoke.

Then the Nāga sent forth flames, and the Blessed One sent forth flames, and he conquered the Nāga, and "leaving intact the skin and flesh and bones of the Nāga, he threw him into his alms bowl (from which he took his daily food) and showed him to Kassapa, saying: 'Here you see the Nāga, his fire has been conquered by my fire.' "[2]

Another wonder was told by Buddha himself to Kassapa, which is given as follows: "I had rags, Kassapa, taken from a dust heap [with which he was going to make himself a robe], and I thought: 'Where shall I wash these rags?' Then Sakka, the king of the devas, understanding the thought which had arisen in my mind, dug a tank with his hand,

[1] The "chief of men," as a term applied to Buddha, is more literally rendered "the snake among men. See Maha-vagga, n. 1. 15, 6.

[2] This account has been greatly condensed. See Maha-vagga, 1, 15, 3.

and said: 'Lord, might the Blessed One wash the rags here?'

"And I thought: 'What shall I rub the rags upon?' Then Sakka put a great stone there and said: 'Lord, might the Blessed One rub the rags upon this stone?'

"And I thought: 'What shall I take hold of when going up out of the tank?'

"Then a deity which resided in a tree bent down a branch, and said: 'Lord, might not the Blessed One take hold of this branch when going up?'

"And I thought: 'Where shall I lay the rags (in order to dry them)?'

"Then Sakka, the king of the devas, put a great stone there, and said: 'Lord, might the Blessed One lay the rags on this stone?'

"Then Kassapa thought: 'Truly the great Saman possesses high magical powers and facilities, since Sakka, the king of the devas, does service to him.'"[1]

GREAT EFFICACY OF RECITATION.

These early texts were repeated over and over again; indeed, the daily life of the monks began with a recitation of the Law, and it was supposed that a talismanic virtue attended the sound of the words.

To illustrate the great meritorious efficacy of the constant intoning of the words, a story is told of five hundred bats that lived together in a cave where two monks performed their daily recitations. These bats gained such merit, by simply hearing the sound, that

[1] Maha-vagga, 1, 20, 1-7.

when they died they were all reborn as men and ultimately as gods.[1]

It is also stated that a certain frog, being fortunate enough to hear Buddha's voice while he was reciting the Law, acquired so much merit thereby that he was born in one of the heavens.[2]

It is faith in the wonderful efficacy of constant repetition which has given birth to the prayer wheels, which are supposed to repeat certain formulas with every revolution of the wheel.

INTEGRITY OF THE TEXT.

In relation to the integrity of the early Pāli texts from which the foregoing quotations are made, the translators express their opinion in the following language:

"Though we must believe that the Vinaya, before it was reduced to writing, was handed down for about three hundred years solely by memory, and that it lived only in the minds of the Bhikkhus, 'who were versed in the Vinaya,' we do not think it is at all necessary, or even possible, to impugn the substantial accuracy of the texts handed down in a manner that seems to moderns so unsafe. The text, as it lies before us, stands so well against all proofs, whether we compare its different parts one with another, or with the little that is yet known of its northern counterparts, that we are justified in regarding these Pāli books, *as in fact the authentic mirror of the old Magadhi text, as fixed in the central schools*

[1] Williams, B., p. 557. [2] Hardy, p. 392.

of the most ancient Buddhist Church."[1] This being true, we must have in these early works the most authentic teachings of Buddha.

We also have in the Vinaya-piṭaka an invaluable and indisputable record of the mental characteristics and capabilities of these earliest followers of the Buddhist faith.

[1] Sa. Bks. E., Vol. XIII, p. xxxvi. (Int.)

CHAPTER IX.

EARLY BUDDHIST LITERATURE, CONTINUED.

THE SECOND PIṬAKA — THE MAHĀ-PARINIBBĀNA SUTTANA — THE PROXIMATE CAUSES OF EARTHQUAKES — THE DHAMMA-PADA — PUNISHMENT — THE SUTTA-NIPĀTA — THE THIRD PIṬAKA — THE MAHĀ-YĀNA, OR NORTHERN SCHOOL — THE BUDDHA-*K*ARITA-KĀVYA — THE SŪTRAS OF JAPAN — THE AMITĀYUR-DHYĀNA — THE VAGRAK-KHEDIKĀ — THE DOCTRINAL TEACHING OF THE SŪTRA — THE PRAGÑĀ-PĀRAMITĀ — THE TĀNTRA LITERATURE — STRIKING CONTRASTS.

THE Second Piṭaka contains the ethical doctrines which first constituted the whole Buddhist law. It is a collection of Sūtras, many of which are themselves composed of smaller works.

The most important of these books are the Mahāparinibbāna Sutta, or Book of the Great Decease; the Dhamma-pada, or Precepts of the Law; the Jātakas, with their commentaries; the Sutta-nipāta, or collection of discourses; the Khuddaka-pāṭha, or short readings, verses by the elder monks, and verses by the elder nuns. We have also the Majjhima, the Sa*m*yutta, the Aṅguttara, and there are others which contain the joyous utterances of Buddha at different crises of his life or treat of his sayings.

One of these minor Suttas treats of the mansions of the gods which move about at will and sometimes descend upon the earth, and another gives information concerning departed spirits.

The Niddesa is a commentary on the Sutta-nipāta; another Sutta treats of the supernatural knowledge of the Arhats, and we have also the Buddha-vaṉsa, or history of the twenty-four Buddhas who preceded Gautama, and of Gautama himself. Another contains stories which are based upon the Jātakas describing Gautama's acquisition of the ten virtues in former births.

THE MAHĀ-PARINIBBĀNA.

This is one of the longest as well as the most valuable of the Suttas, and it is considered one of the oldest parts of the canon except the Pātimokkha. It treats of the death of Buddha and of the events which shortly preceded it, and has, therefore, been considered in connection with that subject.[1] It contains several discourses which he delivered to his followers, some of which have been given in the foregoing pages. As might be supposed, his teachings here were often a repetition of the doctrines which he had previously taught, but his instructions pertained to many subjects. For instance, a short time before his death he explained to Ānanda the cause of earthquakes. The following is his solution of the problem:

THE PROXIMATE CAUSES OF EARTHQUAKES.

"Then the venerable Ānanda went up to the place where the Blessed One was, and did obeisance to the

[1] See pp. 77, 80.

Blessed One, and seated himself respectfully at one side and said: 'Wonderful, indeed, and marvelous is it, that this mighty earthquake should arise. . . . What may be the proximate, what the remote cause of the appearance of this earthquake?'

"Eight are the proximate, eight the remote causes, Ānanda, for the appearance of the mighty earthquake. This great earth, Ānanda, is established on water; the water on wind, and the wind rests upon space. And at such a time, Ānanda, as the mighty winds blow, the waters are shaken by the mighty winds as they blow, and by the moving water the earth is shaken. These are the first causes, proximate and remote, of the appearance of the mighty earthquake.

"Again, Ānanda, a Samaṇa, or a Brāhman of great intellectual power who has the feelings of his heart well under his control, or a god, or a fairy[1] of great or mighty power—when such an one by intense meditation has succeeded in realizing the comparative value of things, he can make this earth move and tremble and be shaken violently.[2] These are the second causes, proximate and remote, of the appearance of a mighty earthquake.

"Again, Ānanda, when a Bodhisat (or future Buddha) consciously and deliberately leaves his temporary

[1] The word here rendered fairy is devata, and the term includes gods of all sorts, tree and river nymphs, the kindly fairies, or ghosts who haunt houses, spirits in the ground, etc.—*Oldenberg and Davids.*

[2] Buddha-ghosha, the Buddhist commentator, tells a long story in relation to this subject, to the effect that the nephew of Naga Thera attained Aratship on the day of his admission to the order. He then proceeded to heaven, and standing on the pinnacle of the palace of the king of the gods he shook the whole place with his great toe, much to the annoyance and consternation of the exalted dwellers therein.—*Sa. Bks. E., Vol. XI, n, p. 46.*

form in the heaven of delight and descends into his mother's womb, then is this earth made to shake and tremble violently. These are the third causes, proximate or remote, of a mighty earthquake.

"Again, Ānanda, when a Bodhisat deliberately and consciously quits his mother's womb, then the earth quakes and is shaken violently. This is the fourth cause, proximate and remote, of the appearance of a mighty earthquake.

"Again, Ānanda, when a Tathāgata (or Buddha) arrives at the supreme and perfect enlightenment, then this earth quakes and is shaken violently. This is the fifth cause, proximate and remote, of a mighty earthquake.

"When a Tathāgata founds a sublime kingdom of righteousness, then this earth . . . is shaken violently. This is the sixth cause, proximate and remote, of a mighty earthquake.

"Again, Ānanda, when a Tathāgata consciously and deliberately rejects the remainder of this life . . . this is the seventh cause . . . of the appearance of a mighty earthquake.

"Again, Ānanda, when a Tathāgata passes entirely away (or dies) with that utter passing away in which nothing whatever is left behind, then this earth . . . is shaken violently. This is the eighth cause of the appearance of a mighty earthquake."[1]

There are several short Suttas of minor importance, some of which have been quoted in the preceding pages, but a much finer literary style, as well as a higher grade of morality, is found in the

[1] Maha-parinibbana Sutta, chap. iii, 2.

DHAMMA-PADA.

It is thought that we now possess this work in very much the same form as it existed in the fifth century of the Christian era, and that the original may have been one of the books which was reduced to writing in the first century before our era, having previously existed in the language of Magadha. And although all Indian manuscripts are comparatively modern,[1] and the chronological evidence concerning them quite uncertain, still these verses may be treated as those which the early Buddhists believed to be the utterances of their founder.

The following extracts will give a good general idea of the teaching which is found in this valuable work:

PUNISHMENT.

"All men tremble at punishment, all men fear death; remember you are like unto them, and do not kill, do not cause slaughter.

"All men tremble at punishment, all men love life; remember thou art like unto them, and do not kill.

"He who seeking his own happiness, punishes or kills beings who also long for happiness, will not find happiness after death.

"He who seeking his own happiness, does not

[1] Mr. A. Burnell, who has probably handled more Indian manuscripts than anybody else, has expressed his conviction that no manuscript written one thousand years ago is now existent in India, and that it is almost impossible to find one written five hundred years ago, for most manuscripts which claim to be of that date are merely copies of old manuscripts, the dates of which are repeated by the copyists.—*Indian Antiquary, 1880, p. 233.*

punish or kill beings who also long for happiness, will find happiness after death.

"Do not speak harshly to anybody; those who are spoken to harshly, will answer thee in the same way. Angry speech is painful, blows for blows will touch thee.

"A fool does not know when he commits evil deeds; but the wicked burns by his own deeds as if burnt by fire.

"He who inflicts pain on innocent and harmless persons, will soon come to one of these ten states. He will have cruel suffering, loss, injury of the body, heavy affliction, or loss of mind, or a misfortune coming from the king, or a fearful accusation, or loss of relations, or destruction of treasures, or lightning fire will burn his houses, and when the body is destroyed the fool will go to hell.

"Not nakedness, not platted (or matted) hair, or lying on the earth; not rubbing with dust, nor sitting motionless, can purify a mortal who has not overcome desires."[1]

The Jātaka and their commentaries have been considered in the foregoing pages and copious extracts have been given.[2]

The Buddha-vaṉsa gives a history of the twenty-four Buddhas who preceded Gautama, and these have been briefly examined.[3]

THE SUTTA-NIPĀTA.

This collection of discourses is an important contribution to the correct understanding of Primitive Bud-

[1] Dhamma-pada, X, 129-141.

[2] See pp. 45, 85, 104.

[3] Twenty-four Buddhas. See chap. ii.

dhism, for we have here a picture of the lives of hermits before monasteries were built.

Buddha here teaches that all family life and all association with others should be avoided.

"As a beast unbound in the forest goes feeding at pleasure, so let the wise man, considering only his own will, wander alone like the rhinoceros."[1] Each of the forty-one verses of one of the Suttas[2] ends with the words: "Let one wander alone like a rhinoceros."

In the Nipāta, Buddha teaches that no one is purified by philosophy or by virtuous works,[3] only by believing in Buddha and in the Dhamma.[4] He must become what Buddha is, and what then is he? Buddha is a visionary in the good sense of the word, that is, his knowledge is intuitive.[5] He is also an ascetic, one who forsakes the home and wanders from house to the houseless state.[6] An ascetic has no prejudiced views,[7] he has shaken off every philosophical view,[8] he is not pleased nor displeased with anything,[9] he is indifferent to learning,[10] he does not cling to good and evil,[11] he has cut off all passion and all desire.[12] He has reached peace, he has gone to the unchangeable state of Nibbāna.[13] This state has been brought about by the destruction of consciousness,[14] by the cessation of sensation,[15] by being without breathing.[16]

Sin, according to this Sutta, is desire in all its

1 Sutta-nipata, verse 38.
2 The Khaggavisana.
3 Nipata, v. 839.
4 vv. 185, 1142.
5 vv. 837, 207.
6 vv 273, 375.
7 v. 802.
8 v. 787.
9 v. 813.
10 v. 911.
11 vv. 520, 547.
12 vv. 2, 795, 916.
13 v. 203.
14 vv. 734, 735.
15 v. 1110.
16 v. 1089.

forms, especially the "thirst for existence,"[1] for name and form — individual existence.[2]

As long as a man is led by desire he will be whirled about in existence,[3] but desire originates in the body, and consequently the human body is looked upon as a contemptible thing, one whole Sutta being devoted to a revolting description of it.[4]

Bliss is emancipation from the body and matter. One must destroy the elements of existence that one may not come to exist again.[5] The wise hold that there is nothing really existing,[6] and those whose minds are disgusted with a future existence, go out like a lamp.[7] As a flame blown out by the wind goes out and cannot be reckoned as existing, even so a Muni, delivered from name and body, disappears and cannot be reckoned as existing.[8]

"Exert thyself, then, being wise and thoughtful in this world, let one having listened to my utterance learn his own extinction."[9]

THE THIRD PIṬAKA.

The third Piṭaka was called the Abhi-dhamma (further dharma), or additional precepts relative to law and philosophy. It is held by modern scholars to be of a later origin and supplementary to the Suttas. It is composed of seven small prose works treating of various subjects. The first is an enumeration of the conditions of existence; the second is devoted to "ex-

[1] v. 1067.
[2] vv. 354, 1099.
[3] v. 740.
[4] See the Vigaya.
[5] vv. 1120, 1122.
[6] v. 1069.
[7] vv. 234, 353, 354.
[8] v. 1073.
[9] v. 1061.

planations;" the third contains "discussions on one thousand controverted points;" the fourth claims to be an explanation of personality; the fifth is an account of the elements; the sixth treats of pairs, and the seventh of causes.

THE MAHĀ-YĀNA, OR NORTHERN SCHOOL.

Besides these numerous works which constitute the Tri-piṭaka, or three collections of works of the Southern Buddhists, there are the Pāli commentaries, which were translated into Singhalese, according to tradition, by Mahendra. Afterward the original Pāli text was lost, and some of the commentaries were retranslated into Pāli by Buddha-ghosha at the end of the fourth and beginning of the fifth century of our era.

The Mahā-yāna, or "Great Vehicle," cannot be said to possess any true canon distinct from the Tri-piṭaka, though some Nepalese Sanskṛit works composed in later times are held to be canonical by Northern Buddhists. The formation of a Northern School, as distinct from the Southern, followed the conversion of Kanishka, the Indo-Scythian king of Kashmīr, who came from the North and became a zealous Buddhist. He probably reigned in the second half of the first century of the Christian era. It was during his reign that a fourth Council was held, which consisted of five hundred monks. These men composed three Sanskṛit works, which were commentaries on the three Pāli piṭakas. These were the earliest books of the Mahā-yāna, or Northern School, which afterward formulated its doctrines on the banks of the Indus, while the

Pāli canon of the South represented the true doctrine promulgated on the Ganges.

Kashmīr was a center of Sanskṛit learning, and Kanishka, who was its patron, sustained to Northern Buddhism about the same relation which Aśoka had borne to the Southern element. Therefore, in time, other books of Northern Buddhism were written in Sanskṛit, with occasional stanzas which were partly in Sanskṛit and partly in Prākṛit.[1]

THE BUDDHA-*k*ARITA-KĀVYA.

This is one of the most important works of the Northern School, and it is claimed that the author was the contemporary and spiritual adviser of Kanishka. It contains an account of the life of Buddha, and is in many points quite in harmony with other Buddhistic works on this subject. For instance, in relation to the conception of Gautama, it is said of him: "Assuming the form of a huge elephant, white like Himālaya, armed with six tusks, with his face perfumed with the flowing ichor, he entered the womb of the queen of king Śuddhodana, to destroy the evils of the world." This work also describes the revolting scene in the harem, which is given by many Buddhistic authorities as a potent influence in deciding Buddha to leave his home. There is no mention here of any farewell look at his wife and child; indeed, his wife is not spoken of at all until the return of the horse and groom, when she joins in the loud wail of the other women, and complains that her husband

[1] Williams, B., p. 68.

left her "helplessly asleep in the night," and even accuses the horse of treachery and dishonorable conduct in bearing him away.

She also here bemoans his great personal beauty, and her description of his person is in harmony with other early accounts. She alludes to his feet in the following language: "Those two feet of his, tender, with their beautiful web spread between the toes . . . how can they (bearing a wheel in the middle) walk on the hard ground of the skirts of the forest?" Here, as elsewhere, she also cites the fact that other monarchs have led faithful religious lives without deserting their families, and expresses a wish to share his penance and privations as others had allowed their wives to do.

"He wishes to practice a religious life after abandoning me, his lawful wife, widowed. Where is his religion, who wishes to follow penance, without his lawful wife to share it with him? . . . He surely never heard of the monarchs of olden time, his own ancestors . . . how they went with their wives into the forest—that he wishes to follow a religious life without me. . . . He does not see that husband and wife are both consecrated in sacrifices . . . and both destined to enjoy the same results afterward—he, therefore, grudges me a share in his merit."[1]

In this [illegible] of the latter part of the first century of the Christian era the temptation of Māra is given, though it is omitted in some earlier texts, and the

[1] Bk., viii, 62, 63.

description of the contest is much like the one which has been given in the foregoing pages.[1]

The Lalita Vistara is also a standard work of the Northern School, but it has been previously considered in connection with the life of Buddha.[2]

THE SŪTRAS OF JAPAN.

A majority of the inhabitants of Japan are Buddhists, and about one-third of these belong to the Shin-shiu sect. The books upon which they found their faith are the two Sukhāvatī-vyūhas, the large and the small, and the Amitāyur-dhyāna-sūtra. They are sometimes called the Large Sūtra, the Small Sūtra, and the Sūtra of Meditation. The same three books also form the chief authority of the *G*ōdoshiu sect.

The followers of this sect claim that in the third century an Indian student came to China and translated the larger of these, and still later[3] another teacher came and translated the other two. The Larger and Smaller Sūtras differ with each other on several points, but the most important variation is found in the fact that the Smaller Sūtra lays great stress on the fact that people can be saved, or can be born in the Land of Bliss, if only they remember and repeat the name of Buddha Amitābha[4] two, three, four or more nights before their death, and it distinctly denies that people are born in the Paradise of Ami-

[1] See p. 56. [2] See p. 44.

[3] In the year 400 A. D. Buddhism was introduced into Japan, by way of Corea, in 552 A. D.

[4] Amitabha was represented by Buddha Gautama as one of the Buddhas who preceded him. (See Larger Sukhavati-vyuha, Int. p. 10.)

tābha as a reward or necessary result of good works performed in this present life.[1]

"This," says Prof. F. Max Müller, "would seem to take away one of the fundamental doctrines of Buddhism, namely, the doctrine of karman, or of the continuous working of our deeds, whether good or bad. . . . The Larger Sūtra also lays great stress on prayer and faith in Amitābha, but it never neglects 'the stock of merit' necessary for salvation. It would almost seem as if this popular and easy doctrine had secured to itself the name of Mahā-yāna, as meaning 'the broad way' in opposition to the Hīna-yāna."[2]

THE AMITĀYUR-DHYĀNA, OR SŪTRA OF MEDITATION.

An outline of this work may be briefly given as follows: "Vaidehī, seeing the wicked actions of her son, began to feel weary of this world. Gautama then taught her how to be born in the pure land, enumerating three kinds of good actions. The first is worldly goodness, which includes good actions in general, such as filial piety, respect of elders, loyalty and faithfulness. The second is the goodness of morality, and all those who do not oppose the general rule of reproving wickedness and exhorting to the practice of virtue are included in this goodness. The third is the goodness of practice, which includes the four truths and the six per-

[1] Sanghavarman's translation of the 18, 20 and 21, is as follows: "When I have attained Buddhahood, if those who are in the ten quarters believe in me and wish to be born in my country, and should have thought of me ten times (or repeated my name), if they should not be born there, may I not obtain perfect knowledge; barring only those who have committed the five deadly sins, and who have spoken evil of the good Law."—*Note by Bunyiu Nanjio, M. A., p. 73.*

[2] Larger Sukhavati-vyuha, Int. p. 9.

fections. Much of this Sūtra is devoted to instructions concerning the proper method of meditation. In relation to Buddha Amitāyus the directions are as follows:

"Further, when this perception is gained, you should next proceed to meditate on the bodily marks[1] and the light of Buddha Amitāyus.

"Thou shouldst know, O Ānanda, that the body of Buddha Amitāyus is a hundred thousand million times as bright as the color of the gold of the heavenly abode of Yama. The height of that Buddha is six hundred thousand niyutas of koṭis[2] of yojanas, innumerable as are the sands of the river Gangā.

"The white twist of hair between the eyebrows, all turning to the right, is just like the five Sumēru mountains.

"The eyes of Buddha are like the water of the four great oceans.

"All the roots of hair of his body issue forth brilliant rays which are also like the Sumēra mountains.

"The halo of that Buddha is like a hundred million of niyutas of koṭis, innumerable as the sands of the Gangā; each of these Buddhas has for attendants a great assembly of numberless Bodhisattas, who are also miraculously created.

"Buddha Amitāyus has eighty-four thousand signs of perfection, each sign is possessed of eighty-four minor marks of excellence, each mark has eighty-four

[1] All the Buddhas were possessed of these bodily marks of perfection. See page 48.

[2] The numbers in Buddhist literature, when they exceed a koti or ten millions, become very vague, nor is their value always the same. Ayuta represents a hundred kotis; niyuta represents a hundred ayutas. (See Smaller Sukhavati-vyuha, p. 91.) A yojana, four or more miles.

thousand rays, each ray extends so far as to shine over the worlds of the ten quarters, whereby Buddha embraces and protects all the beings who think upon him, and does not exclude any."[1]

THE VAGRAKKHEDIKĀ OR DIAMOND CUTTER.

This is a metaphysical treatise, and it is one of the most highly valued works in Buddhist literature. The name has sometimes been rendered "The Perfection of Wisdom." The Tibetans value it very highly, and many copies have been made.

"Translated literally into English," says F. Max Müller, "it must often strike the reader as sheer nonsense and hollow repetition.

"Nor can anything be said in defense of the form or style adopted in this treatise by the Buddhist philosophers, who wished to convince their hearers of the truth of their philosophy. This philosophy, or, at least, its underlying doctrine, is not unknown to us. It is simply a denial of the reality of the phenomenal world."[2]

The doctrine of metaphysics, which is here taught, has been presented in the foregoing pages,[3] and the value placed upon these Gāthās may be learned from the following extract:

"Bhagavat said: 'What do you think, O Subhûti, if there were as many Gangā rivers as there are grains of sand in the large river Gangā, would the grains of sand be many?'

"Subhûti said: 'Those Gangā rivers would, indeed,

[1] Amitayur-dhyana-sutra, Sec. 18.
[2] Int. Vagrakkhedika, p. 14.
[3] See p. 184.

be many, much more, the grains of sand in those Gangā rivers.'

"Bhagavat said: 'I tell you, O Subhūti! I announce to you if a man or woman were to fill with the seven treasures, as many worlds as there would be grains of sand in those Gangā rivers, and present them as a gift to the holy Tathāgatas; what do you think, O Subhūti! would that man or woman, on the strength of this, produce a large stock of merit?'

"Subhūti said: 'Yes, O Bhagavat, that man or that woman would, on the strength of this, produce a large stock of merit, immeasurable and innumerable.'

"Bhagavat said: 'And if, O Subhūti, a woman or man, having filled so many worlds with the seven treasures, should give them as a gift to the holy and enlightened Tathāgatas, and if another son or daughter of a good family, after taking from this treatise of the Law one Gāthā of four lines only, should fully teach others and explain it, he, indeed, would, on the strength of tnis, produce a larger stock of merit, immeasurable and innumerable.' "[1]

DOCTRINAL TEACHING OF THE SŪTRA.

The metaphysics which form the basis of the teaching of this work may be better understood from the following extract:

"O Bhagavat, knowledge has been produced in me. Never, indeed, O Bhagavat, has such a teaching of the Law been heard by me before. Those Bodhisattas will be endowed with the highest wonder[2] who, when

[1] Vagrakkhedika, XI.

[2] Will possess miraculous powers and will be admired.

this Sūtra is being preached, hear it, and will frame to themselves a true idea. And why? Because what is a true idea, is not a true idea. . . . But, O Bhagavat, there will not arise in them any idea of a self, any idea of a being, of a living being, or a person, nor does there exist for them any idea or no idea. And why? Because the blessed Buddhas are freed from all ideas.' . . .

"O Subhūti, I remember the past five hundred births when I was a preacher of endurance. At that time also I had no idea of a self, of a being, of a living being, of a person.

"Therefore, then, O Subhūti, a noble-minded Bodhisatta, after putting aside all ideas, should raise his mind to the highest perfect knowledge.

"He should frame his mind so as not to believe in form, sound, smell, taste, or anything that can be touched, in something, in nothing, or anything.

"And why? Because what is believed, is not believed. Therefore, the Tathāgata preaches: 'A gift should not be given by one who believes in form, sound, smell, taste, or anything that can be touched.'"[1]

THE PRAGÑĀ-PĀRAMITĀ (TRANSCENDENT WISDOM).

The Sūtra, although very brief, is said to be really the most popular and one of the most important of all the sacred texts upon which Buddhism takes its stand in Japan. This treatise of the Law is to be seen everywhere on shrines, temples and monasteries,

[1] Vagrakkhedika, XIV.

although probably more admired than understood by the masses of the people. The same eulogy is pronounced upon its value as that previously given in relation to the Diamond-cutter, and in nearly the same language. Although it is spoken of in the singular number, it is really composed of two Sūtras, the larger and the smaller.

As they both teach the same doctrine of metaphysics, and the smaller merely repeats the ideas of the other, the following extract from the larger will give a very definite idea of both:

"If the son or daughter of a family wishes to perform the study of the deep Pra*g*ñā-pāramitā, he must think thus: 'There are five Skandhas,[1] and these, he considered by their nature, empty. Form is emptiness, and emptiness, indeed, is form. . . . What is form, that is emptiness; what is emptiness, that is form. . . .

"Thus, O Sāriputra, all things have the character of emptiness . . . they are faultless, and not faultless; they are not imperfect, and not perfect. Therefore, here in emptiness there is no form, no perception, no eye, ear, nose, body, mind. . . .

[1] Every being is composed of five constituent elements, called Skandhas, and these are continually combining, dissolving and recombining. They are: 1. Form (the organized body). 2. Sensation. 3. Perception. 4. Aggregate of formations (a combination of properties, faculties or mental tendencies, fifty-two in number). 5. Consciousness or thought. This is the most important, and is the only soul recognized by Buddhists. It was this view which enabled Buddha to teach transmigration while denying the existence of any spirit separate from the body, for although when a man dies all these elements are dissolved, yet by the force resulting from his actions, combined with the sin of "clinging to existence," a new set of five, of which consciousness is still the dominant faculty, starts into being, and a new creature is immediately created.

There is no knowledge, no obtaining, or not obtaining of Nirvāṇa. But when the envelopment of *consciousness* has been annihilated, then he becomes free from all fear, beyond the reach of change, enjoying the final Nirvāṇa."[1]

THE TĀNTRA LITERATURE.

"The Tāntra literature has also had its growth and development, and some unhappy scholar of a future age may have to trace its loathsome history. . . . The nauseous taste repelled even the self-sacrificing industry of Burnouf when he found the later Tāntra books to be as immoral as they were absurd. 'The pen,' he says, 'refuses to transcribe doctrines as miserable in respect to form as they are odious and degrading in respect to meaning.'"[2]

STRIKING CONTRASTS.

There is probably no other collection of sacred books in the world which presents such peculiar and forcible contrasts as do those of Buddhism. Scholars have repeatedly noted "the feeble utterances, the tedious diffuseness, and, I might almost say, the 'inane twaddle' and childish repetitions of the greater portion of the Tri-piṭaka,"[3] while, on the other hand, the Dhamma-pada and portions of some other books contain gems of thought and beauty of expression which will compare favorably with the literary stand-

[1] Larger Pragna-paramita.

[2] Rhys Davids, B., p. 208. Burnouf, Int. p. 588. The secret Tantric doctrines are found in the seventh division of the enumeration of the nine Nepalese canonical scriptures.

[3] See Williams, B., p. 558; also Max Müller (Int. Vagrakkhedika, p. 14), and many others.

ards of any people. The contrast is forcible, not only in relation to the style of the books in question, but there is also a pure literature and that which is notably impure.[1] We find in some of the books of Buddhism an exalted morality, and admonitions to purity of thought, word and deed. These works also inculcate the duties of charity, self-sacrifice and benevolence.

It is entirely natural for the author as well as the reader to seek for these gems alone and display them freely to others. But a wrong impression is usually conveyed by presenting only one side of a question, and careful writers must avoid this mistake, which too many have made, unconsciously, perhaps, to themselves.

Therefore, some brave historian of the future must wade through the revolting horrors of the Pārājika books, and give also an exposition of the odious doctrines which Burnouf and others could not bring themselves to transcribe. These things, however, should always be kept strictly within the pale of critical scholarship, for the world has no need of them. The problem which requires explanation is the existence of such doctrines in a sacred literature.

Why should the same canon contain works which differ so greatly in literary style and in teaching, as do the texts of the Tri-piṭaka and the Dhamma-pada, with its classic beauty and pure morality?

Why should the Tāntra literature and the unmentionable ceremonies of Śiva worship find a place in the same system of philosophy with "the noble eightfold path?"

[1] See p. 149.

CHAPTER X.

EARLY BUDDHIST LITERATURE, CONCLUDED.

BUDDHA'S INDEBTEDNESS TO BRĀHMANISM — THE DHAMMA-PADA — SIMILARITIES TO OLD TESTAMENT TEACHINGS — POSSIBLE SOURCES OF INFORMATION — SUMMARY.

THE striking contrasts which Buddhism presents both in morals and literature are worthy of more than a passing notice, and the faithful student must inquire whence they came.

Prof. F. Max Müller has repeatedly pointed out the fact that the Buddhists are indebted to the Brāhmans for almost all of their philosophical speculations,[1] and it should also be noted that, even in the choice of a name derived from the Sanskṛit root *budh,* the Buddha adopted the phraseology of the Sāṅkhya philosophy and of the Brāhmans. The Sāṅkhya system made Buddhi (intellect) its great principle, and the Śatapatha-brāhmaṇa called a man who had attained to perfect knowledge of Self, prati-buddha.[2]

Again, the doctrines which grew out of his own special knowledge, Gautama called Dharma[3] (law),

[1] Prof. F. Max Müller, Int. Amitayur-dhyana-sutra, p. 22. Sa. Bks. E., Vol. XLIX.

[2] XIV, 7, 2, 17. This was first pointed out by Prof. A. Weber.

[3] Dharma or Dhamma.

using the same term which was employed by the Brāhmans.

Buddha's "way of knowledge," though it developed into many paths, was primarily a knowledge of the truth that all life was merely one link in a series of successive existences and inseparably bound up with misery, and this extreme pessimism, which was the fundamental doctrine of Buddhism, was taught by the Brāhmans five centuries before Christ, and it continued to be a thoroughly Hindū doctrine long after the disappearance of Buddhism from India.

Indeed, all Indian philosophy was a scheme for getting rid of the ceaseless round of existence, which was taught in the doctrine of metempsychosis, and annihilation was looked upon as a welcome deliverance.

In India the Upanishads, and the systems of philosophy which followed them, were all attuned to this same minor key, the real object of the authors being the discovery of a plan for removing the misery which they believed to result from repeated bodily existence, and from all action, good or bad, in the present, previous, and future births.

Gautama's adherence to these ideas is repeatedly shown in his teaching. He had a way, however, of clothing old ideas in a new dress, which proved very attractive to his followers, and he rejected, too, some of the radical ideas of the Upanishads, although his sympathy with much of their teaching was very strong.

The term Nirvāṇa, for instance, was not original with Gautama; it was an expression which was common to both Brāhmanism and Buddhism, and most of its synonyms are still common to both; nevertheless, he gave a different shade to the meaning of the word, for he could not advocate that it meant "the extinction in the Supreme Being"[1] of those who attained Nirvāṇa, while he refused to admit the existence of such a Being.

THE DHAMMA-PADA

This work, which is the most valuable of all the Buddhistic writings, also contains within itself some striking contrasts and inculcates ideas which are apparently derived from very different sources.

"By earnestness did Indra rise to the lordship of the gods."[2] This verse, and all others which contain allusions to this deity, must be of Brāhmanic origin, for Indra was the Jove of early Indian mythology. He is represented as being the king of the celestial beings who occupy his paradise, although after one hundred years of the gods, another, and possibly a man, may by great sacrifices usurp his position.

"Without ceasing, I shall run through the course of many births."[3] This sentiment is also in accordance with the doctrine of transmigration, which was taught in both Egypt and India long before Gautama's time.

Again, we find the following statement: "The man who wears dirty garments, who is emaciated, who lives alone in the forest and meditates, him I call,

[1] This doctrine was taught in the Upanishads, and later in the Bhagavadgita (v. 24).

[2] Dhamma-pada, v. 30.

[3] Dhamma, v. 395.

indeed, a Brāhmaṇa." Here is an endorsement of the asceticism which was practiced under the dominion of Brāhmanism, and also by Buddha and some of his followers.

But while these and many others are evidently of purely Hindū origin, there are others which are very different.

SIMILARITIES TO OLD TESTAMENT TEACHINGS.

Many of the most valuable of these precepts will be found to be almost identical in sentiment with proverbs which Solomon uttered about five hundred years before the birth of Buddha. From a multitude of forcible illustrations of this statement we select a few:

"For hatred does not cease by hatred at any time; hatred ceases by love; this is an old rule."[1]

The "old rule," however, had been more tersely expressed in Proverbs, where it is said that "Hatred stirreth up strifes, but love covereth all sins."[2]

Again, in the Dhamma-pada it is said: "The evil doer suffers in this world, and he suffers in the next. He suffers when he thinks of the evil he has done, he suffers more when going on the evil path."[3]

This sentiment had been more eloquently expressed by the prophet Isaiah in the words: "The wicked are like the troubled sea when it cannot rest, whose waters cast up mire and dirt. There is no peace, saith my God, to the wicked."[4]

In the Dhamma-pada it is said: "Thoughtlessness

[1] Dhamma, v. 5.
[2] Proverbs, x, 12.
[3] Dhamma, v. 17.
[4] Isaiah, lvii, 20-21.

is the path of death. Those who reflect do not die—those who are thoughtless are dead already."[1]

This idea had been expressed in Proverbs as follows: "In the way of righteousness is life, and in the pathway thereof there is no death."[2]

Again, in the Buddhist work it is said: "If an earnest person has aroused himself, if he is not forgetful, if his deeds are pure, if he acts with consideration . . . then his glory shall increase."[3]

The Psalmist, however, had written: "He that walketh uprightly, and worketh righteousness, and speaketh the truth in his heart . . . he that doeth these things shall never be moved."[4]

The Dhamma-pada says: "Fools follow after vanity, the wise man keeps earnestness as his best jewel."[5]

Solomon had previously written: "The crown of the wise is their riches, but the foolishness of fools is their folly."[6]

In the Dhamma-pada we find the admonition: "Follow not after vanity, nor after the enjoyment of love and lust."[7]

The Psalmist had previously enquired: "How long will ye love vanity and seek after leasing?"[8]

In the sayings of Buddha we find the following: "If a traveler does not meet with one who is his equal, let him keep to his solitary journey; there is no companionship with a fool."[9]

Solomon had, however, expressed the sentiment more

[1] Dhamma, v. 21.
[2] Prov., xii, 28.
[3] Dhamma, v. 34.
[4] Psalms, xv, 2, 5.
[5] Dhamma, v. 26.
[6] Proverbs, xiv, 24.
[7] Dhamma, v. 27.
[8] Psalms, iv, 2.
[9] Dhamma, v. 61.

forcibly when he said: "Let a bear robbed of her whelps meet a man, rather than a fool in his folly."[1]

Buddha said: "A fool who knoweth his foolishness is wise, at least so far."[2]

In Proverbs it had been said: "Even a fool, when he holdeth his peace, is counted wise."[3]

In the Dhamma-pada we find the wise admonition: "Do not have evil doers for friends, do not have low people, have virtuous people for friends."[4]

The Psalmist had previously written: "Blessed is the man that walketh not in the counsel of the ungodly, nor standeth in the way of sinners, nor sitteth in in the seat of the scornful."[5] And Solomon had declared: "He that walketh with wise men shall be wise, but the companion of fools shall be destroyed."[6]

Again, it is stated in the Dhamma-pada: "If one man conquers in battle a thousand times a thousand men, and if another conquer himself, he is the greatest of conquerers."[7]

This verse appears to be almost a repetition of the statement that "He that ruleth his spirit is greater than he that taketh a city."[8]

The saying of Buddha: "The wicked man burns by his own deeds, as if burnt by fire,"[9] reminds one forcibly of the question in Proverbs concerning sin: "Can a man take fire in his bosom and his clothes not be burned? Can one go upon hot coals and his feet not be burned?"[10]

1 Proverbs, xvii, 12.
2 Dhamma, v. 63.
3 Proverbs, xvii, 28.
4 Dhamma, v. 78.
5 Psalms, i, 1.
6 Proverbs, xiii, 20.
7 Dhamma, v. 103.
8 Proverbs, xvi, 32.
9 Dhamma, v. 36.
10 Prov., vi, 27-28.

In the Dhamma-pada it is said: "He who always greets and reveres the aged, four things increase unto him, life, beauty, happiness and power."[1] This is a strange sentiment to find in a system which taught that all life was misery, that beauty and happiness were to be shunned and power ignored. But centuries before Buddha, Moses had written: "Thou shalt rise up before the hoary head and honor the face of the old man."[2]

In the Dhamma-pada it is said: "Do not kill, nor cause slaughter;"[3] but it had long before been written upon tables of stone: "Thou shalt not kill."[4]

In the precepts of Buddha we find the wise admonition: "Do not speak harshly to anybody. Those who are spoken to harshly will answer thee in the same way."[5] This sentiment had been more briefly stated in these words: "A soft answer turneth away wrath, but grievous words stir up anger."[6]

In the Dhamma-pada it is said: "He who dwells in the law, delights in the law, meditates in the law, follows the law, will never fall away from the true law."[7] This is almost a repetition of the words of the Psalmist: "His delight is in the law of the Lord, and in his law doth he meditate day and night."[8]

In the precepts of Buddha it is said: "If a man hold himself dear, let him watch himself carefully."[9] This appears to be an echo of the admonition to

[1] Dhamma, v. 109.
[2] Lev., xix, 32.
[3] Dhamma, v. 129.
[4] Exodus, xx, 13.
[5] Dhamma, v. 133.
[6] Prov., xv, 1.
[7] Dhamma, v. 364.
[8] Psalms, i, 2.
[9] Dhamma, v. 157.

"Take heed to thyself and keep thy soul diligently."[1] and many similar passages.

In the Dhamma-pada it is said: "The fault of others is easily perceived, but that of one's self is difficult to perceive."[2]

This is the same sentiment found in Proverbs: "Every way of a man is right in his own eyes, . . his neighbor findeth no favor in his eyes."[3]

Again, in the Dhamma-pada it is said: "All men tremble at punishment; all men love life; remember that thou art like unto them, and do not kill, nor cause slaughter."[4]

Not only is this injunction preceded by the commandment that "Thou shalt not kill," but the whole sentiment had been more forcibly and broadly expressed hundreds of years before Buddha was born, in the command: "Thou shalt love thy neighbor as thyself."[5]

It has been freely charged that Christ borrowed "the golden rule" from Buddha, or from Confucius, regardless of the fact that the sentiment expressed in Matthew is ascribed "to the law and the prophets."[6]

Many other similarities might be cited between the verses of the Dhamma-pada and the older literature of the Hebrews,[7] but it can hardly be claimed that even these are accidental.

It is certain that every moral principle which has

1 Deut., iv, 9, also Prov., iv, 23.
2 Dhamma, v. 352.
3 Proverbs, xxi, 2, 10.
4 Dhamma, v. 252.
5 Lev., xix, 18.
6 Matthew, vii, 12.
7 Compare especially Dhamma, 34, with Psalms, xv, 2, 5, and Dhamma, 66, with Prov., xviii, 7. Again, compare Dhamma, 69, with Eccl., viii, 2; also Dhamma, 82, with Psalms, cxix, 165, and Isaiah, xlvii, 18, and many others.

been inculcated by either Buddha or his followers was freely taught by Moses and the prophets long before the birth of Gautama.

It is true that Buddhism has ten commandments, the first four of which are virtually the same as those belonging to the Mosaic decalogue,[1] but this fact need not be considered, as it is a circumstance which might easily happen. It is more significant, however, that a story is found in the Jātakas which is apparently based upon the wise decision of Solomon. "The Hebrew story," says Rhys Davids, "in which a similar judgment is ascribed to Solomon, occurs in the book of Kings, which is more than a century older than the time of Gautama . . . and it should be remembered that the chronicle in question was based, for the most part, on tradition current much earlier among the Jewish people, and probably on earlier documents."[2] Not only does it appear very possible that Buddhism has been indebted to the earlier writings, but there are some things, even in Brāhmanism, which would indicate that there may have been some connection between the people of India and the Jews. For instance, the Hindū temple is on the same plan as the tabernacle in the wilderness, and scholars are asking whence the Hindūs can have derived this plan?

Not only this, but Surgeon-General Gordon, in his able paper before the Victoria Institute, or Philosophical Society of Great Britain, on the "Philosophy and Medical Knowledge of Ancient India," has cited a

[1] See p. 125.

[2] B. B. S., Int. pp. xvi, xlv.

great number of points in which the Code of Manu is found to be almost identical with the much earlier Mosaic Code.[1]

When a book presents many ideas which are nearly identical with those of another, it is customary, in the world of letters, to decide who has done the borrowing merely upon the question of chronological precedence. It may be well, however, to briefly consider some of the points of contact between the two nations.

POSSIBLE SOURCES OF INFORMATION.

It was formerly believed that little, if any, intercourse took place between the Semitic and Aryan peoples in early times, but later discoveries have shown that commerce, and even political and literary relations, obtained to a much greater extent than the scholars of the last century supposed.[2] Phœnicia has been found to be the connecting link between Palestine and Greece, both in architecture and art. Not only is this true of Greece, but of other countries as well. The presence of teak at Mugheir proves that the commerce of Babylonia extended as far as India, and Professor Sayce also claims that before the sixth century before Christ the Phœnicians had penetrated to the northwestern coast of India, and her pearls and ivories flowed into their harbors.[3] It will be remembered, too, that Solomon was indebted to Phœnicia for his active commerce with India, and during the building of the temple the fleets of Hiram and Solo-

[1] Surgeon-General Gordon, M. D., C. B., Q. H. P. (Trans. Vic. Inst., Vol. XXV, No. 99.)

[2] See note to p. 153.

[3] Sayce, An. Emp., pp. 176, 181, 208.

mon brought from Ophir[1] gold and precious stones, and abundance of algum trees.[2] There is also reason to believe that there was a great commerce by land between the East and West by way of Palmyra and Mesopotamia. "Though intercourse by sea," says Rhys Davids, "was not continued after Solomon's time, the gold of Ophir, ivory, jade and Eastern gems still continued to find their way to the West; and it would be an interesting task for an Assyrian or Hebrew scholar to trace the evidence of this overland route in other ways."[3]

"Nor should we," says Prof. Max Müller, "when looking for channels of communication between the ancient kingdoms of Asia, forget the Jews, who were more or less at home in every part of the world. We must remember that they came originally from Ur of

1 It is true there is some difference of opinion in reference to the locality of Ophir, but the commerce was of long continuance, and the navies of Solomon and Hiram came once in every three years, "bringing gold and silver, ivory, apes and peacocks." Every one of these are distinctively Indian products, and Professor Lassen considers it unnecessary to examine conjectures concerning other localities, from the fact that products which are said to come from Ophir have Indian names, even in the Hebrew text, when they are destitute of genuine Hebrew names.

In the Septuagint, the translators have invariably rendered the word Ophir, as Souphir, in its various forms, and, according to Coptic lexicographers, Soupher is the general name applied by the Copts to India and its islands.

Josephus says that Solomon's fleets had India for their goal (Ant. vi, 4). See also Professor Sayce (An. Emp., p. 189) and Rhys Davids (B. B. S., Int., p. xlvi); also Carl Von Ritter, the eminent German geographer (Geog. Pal., Vol. I, pp. 116, 126; also Reland (Dissertatio de Ophir), Vitringa (Geog. Sacra., p. 114), Thenius (Exeget. Handbuch, I Kings, x, 22), Bertheau (Exeget. Handbuch, 2 Chron., viii, 18) and Ewald (Geschichte, III, 347, 2d edition).

2 Almug or algum trees furnished the peculiar wood which was used for the terraces of the temple, and it is defined as being "the red sandal wood of India . . . hard, heavy, close grained and of a fine red color."—*Cyclopædia Britannica.*

3 Rhys Davids (B. B. S., xlvii).

the Chaldees, then migrated to Canaan, and afterward sojourned in Egypt before they settled in Palestine. After this, we know they were led into captivity, and lived in close proximity and held daily intercourse with Medians, Persians, Babylonians and Assyrians."[1] Not only is it true that India was one of the provinces of Darius at the time when the prophet Daniel held a high position at the king's court, but later events show that the Jews were very numerous in India during the life of Buddha. Ahasuerus, who "reigned from India even unto Ethiopia," has been definitely identified as Xerxes I.[2] He was contemporary with Buddha,[3] and during his reign the Jews were so numerous in India and the other provinces of his dominion that they made a successful stand against their enemies when the king instructed them to do so. And the great victory which was then obtained was celebrated by the institution of the annual feast of Purim, which is observed by the Jewish people even to this day.[4] Therefore the Jewish people must have been exceedingly numerous in and around India during the time of Buddha, and it is a well known fact that they carried their sacred books, their system

[1] Max Müller, Inaugural Address before the Ninth International Congress of Orientalists.

[2] In a recent letter to the author on this subject, Prof. A. H. Sayce says: "Ahasuerus and Xerxes are the same name, and there is only one Xerxes to whom the account in the book of Esther can refer. That is the famous Xerxes I. Thanks to the decipherment of the cuneiform inscriptions, we now know that the Persian kings did not have two names, so that the old attempt to identify the Xerxes of Esther with Darius or Artaxerxes can never be renewed."

[3] Xerxes came to the throne about 485 B. C.

[4] Esther, ix, 26-32. It is a well known fact that no historic evidence is considered so strong as the existence of the annual celebration of an event,

of ethics and their form of worship into every country where they obtained a foothold. Hence, opportunities were apparently abundant for Buddha and his contemporaries to learn the proverbs and oft-repeated sayings of this peculiar people. If it be true, as Max Müller asserts, that "the Indian alphabet certainly came from a Semitic alphabet,"[1] we may well believe that the alphabet was not the only literary heritage which the people of India received from the Semites.

SUMMARY.

In relation to this department of letters, we have seen that it found its origin at a time when there was a general intellectual activity throughout the East, and the official canon of the Buddhist church is supposed to date from the first century before Christ.

The "three baskets" which compose this canon contain all which refers to morality in these books, and also the discourses of Buddha on various subjects, as well as his definite instructions to monks in reference to the trivial affairs of life. They contain, too, works which treat upon a variety of subjects, including philosophy and discipline. The Law required

and hence the faithful keeping of the Purim feast has added greatly to the weight of testimony in this department of history.

The Talmud is composed of the Mishna and Gemera. The former is the text and the latter is the commentary upon it.

The composers of the Mishna were men belonging to the Sanhedrin many years before the destruction of Jerusalem. There is one section of the Talmud, called the Megillah (scroll), which treats of the book of Esther, the feast of Purim, etc. The Megillah Esther is read by the Hebrews on the day of the Purim feast. *There is no doubt but it was written in Persia, as it contains many Persian words*, and it is ascribed to the time of Artaxerxes Longimanus, who was the son and successor of Xerxes I, and who came to the throne about 465 B. C.

[1] Max Müller, Inaugural Address, p. 29.

that these early texts should be constantly recited, and great merit was accumulated thereby. The phraseology of the Vinaya is thought to be substantially accurate, even though it was long handed down by memory, and, therefore, we have here an invaluable record of the mental characteristics of the early Buddhists.

We have seen, too, that there are strange contrasts in the literature of Buddhism — that while the greater part of the sacred canon abounds with tedious diffuseness and may be considered almost without literary merit, there are other portions which present not only a desirable code of ethics, but also much poetry of expression. While the greater part of this teaching is burdened with luxuriant imagination and crowded with absurd statements, still there is much which is so greatly superior to this that the careful student is forced to the conclusion that the conflicting elements were derived from very different sources. It is impossible to think of the moral horrors of the Tāntra literature as emanating from the same source with the simple beauty of the Dhamma-pada, neither can one conceive of the revolting ceremonies of Śiva worship as a component part of any system of ethics. These forcible antagonisms must be explained in some way, and the most natural conclusion is that they were derived from the various races with whom the Buddhists have come in contact.

Beginning with a simple pessimistic declaration, Buddhism has, in later times, branched out into a great number of complicated and self-contradictory propositions "Its teaching," says Williams, "has become both negative and positive, agnostic and gnostic. It passes from atheism and materialism to theism, polytheism and spiritualism.

"It is, under one aspect, mere pessimism; under another, pure philanthropy; under another, monastic communism; under another, high morality; under another, a variety of materialistic philosophy; under another, simple demonology; under another, a mere farrago of superstitions, including necromancy, witchcraft, idolatry and fetishism. In some form or another, it may be held with almost any religion, and embraces something from almost every creed. It is founded upon philosophical Brāhmanism, has much in common with Sāṅkhya and Vedānta ideas, is closely connected with Vaishṇavism, and in some of its phases with both Śaivism and Śāktism, and yet it is, properly speaking, opposed to every one of these systems."[1] The readiness with which this system allies itself with the leading idea of every people whom it approaches has been frequently noted, so much so that it has been called the "universal borrower," and when upon American soil it even claims some of the doctrines of Christianity. This inveterate tendency for borrowing must account for the numerous inconsistencies which obtain in its teachings and literature.

[1] Williams, B., p. 13.

CHAPTER XI.

CONCLUSION.

PRIMITIVE BUDDHISM IN INDIA — ORIGIN OF THE SYSTEM — ATHEISM — TRANSMIGRATION — KARMA — PESSIMISM — METAPHYSICS — THE ACCUMULATION OF MERIT — NIRVĀṆA — LITERATURE — ORIGINALITY OF BUDDHA — CAUSES OF EXTENSIVE INFLUENCE.

WE have seen that Buddhism, so long as it remained in its primitive form, was a blessing to India, because it encouraged benevolence, self-sacrifice, tolerance and humanity — because it opposed the tyranny of the Brāhmanic priesthood and deprecated war between nations.

In its earliest phase it was not a religion, but merely a system of philosophy which was founded upon extreme pessimism; still, it promoted, to a certain extent, intellectual and moral progress. It taught respect for life and compassion toward the lower animals.

It was a benefit to woman, even though it made war upon the home, because it gave her some semblance of equality by allowing her to become a nun under much the same rules which obtained in communities of men. Although it was claimed that she could never attain perfection except by becoming a man, and although during the reign of Buddhism in India living women were burned upon the dead bodies of their husbands,[1] still this system advocates a certain amount of social freedom. It does not require the imprisonment of wives and daughters in the harem, and the marriage of very young children is not enforced.

We have noted that, although some ideas may have been obtained from other races, the metaphysical and speculative doctrines of Buddhism have found their origin upon Indian soil and in the earlier creeds of the Hindūs. Even points which were thoroughly antagonistic to the Vedic philosophy indicate that they could not have existed without their predecessor.

While Gautama denied the existence of a Creator and repudiated the Veda and all Vedic sacrifices, still he made the philosophy of the Brāhmans the point of departure for his own teaching.

The Sāṅkhya philosophy, in its original form, claims the name of "lordless" or "atheistic" as its distinctive title, but while Buddha's whole system of negation was founded upon atheism, he still recognized the various gods of the Hindū pantheon. And his followers became the worshipers of "lords many, and gods many," to such an extent that more idols are found in Buddhist countries than among any other people.

[1] Unknown thousands of lives were sacrificed in this barbarous manner, as hundreds and sometimes thousands of women were burned alive every year. At the close of the last century seventy widows were burned upon the funeral pyre of one raja.

The horrible custom had obtained in India ever since the days of Alexander until abolished by the English government in the early part of the present century.

We have seen that the doctrine of metempsychosis was promulgated by Egyptian and Hindū for centuries before the birth of Gautama. In the Upanishads[1] (which contain the doctrinal portion of the Veda), we find that the Indian philosophers attempted to devise some plan, or theory, whereby the eternal cycle of existence in constant migration could be avoided.

It remained, however, for Buddha to teach the transmigration of character, and, in some cases, the transfer of consciousness, even while ignoring the existence of a soul.

In immediate connection with the theory of metempsychosis we have found the doctrine that the effect of good or bad actions extended from former lives to the present, and from the present to all future existences. But we meet with these ideas everywhere in the poetry, the philosophy and the religion of the Hindūs; they cannot be claimed as the property of any particular system. There is no forgiveness in the doctrine of karma; a man is bound hand and foot by the inevitable consequences of his own evil actions.

Even the extreme pessimism of Buddha was taught in the doctrinal portion of the Vedas. The Upanishads and other important works were replete with the doctrine that everything was for the worst in

[1] The doctrine of transmigration is found in the first of the series of the Upanishads, and sometimes there is a curious consistency in the various changes—for instance, the man who has stolen perfumery becomes a musk-rat; one who has stolen grain becomes a rat; one who has stolen water becomes a water-fowl; one who has stolen meat becomes a vulture; one who has stolen oil becomes a cockroach, etc.

Although the Upanishads, as such, were not formulated until about the time of Buddha, their doctrines originated much earlier.

this, the worst of all possible worlds.[1] Therefore, Buddha started out with the idea that the highest object to be attained is the escape from pain. Life, in his eyes, was only suffering, and birth was the cause of all evil, from which even death could not deliver him, because of transmigration. There was no deliverance from evil except by breaking through the prison walls of continued life and by extirpating the last cause of existence.

In relation to metaphysics the old Vedānta philosophers thought they were free when they arrived at the knowledge that nothing existed but Brāhman—that all phenomena are merely the result of ignorance. But Buddha pushed the doctrine of negation still farther, and claimed that there is no reality anywhere, neither in the past nor in the future. "True wisdom consists in perceiving the nothingness of all things, and in a desire to become nothing, 'to be blown out,' to enter into Nirvāṇa. Emancipation is obtained by total extinction. . . . If to be, is misery, then not to be, must be felicity, *and this is the highest reward that Buddha offered to his disciples.*"[2]

Buddha had no conception of sin as an offense against God. He taught his followers to get rid of the demerit of evil action and accumulate a stock of merit by good actions. This, too, was a genuine Hindū idea. It is even now the vital portion of Brāhmanism and Hindūism, as well as Zoroastrianism and Confucianism.

[1] See the Maitrayani Upanishad. Also Bhartri-hari, Vairagya-sataka, III, 32, 50.

[2] F. Max Müller, Chips, Vol. I, p. 227.

It is even more vital to Buddhism, as there is no forgiveness in this system, and good actions are represented as the only counterpoise of evil conduct. Hence we find that great sacrifice is required in order to produce great merit, and people made a practice of buying birds (which had been caught by professional bird-catchers for that purpose) and giving them their liberty. Those who were to become Buddhas gave away their wives and their children "to serve others," and the Buddha who received more radiance than any of the others was he who gave his children to be eaten by a demon, while the father looked contentedly on as they were "devoured like a bunch of roots."[1]

It was a system of balancing up accounts, and counteracting by such "good actions" the great accumulation of demerit which had obtained in consequence of the evil actions, not only of the present life but of all the previous forms of existence.

We have seen, too, that Nirvāṇa was not original with Buddha. It occurred also in the literature of the Brāhmans, as a synonym of "deliverance," "cessation" and "release."[2] Brāhmanism had a confused idea that the human soul might be absorbed into the Universal Spirit,[3] but Buddhism could not unite the soul,

[1] See Rhys Davids (B. B. S., p. 33).

[2] Different views of Nirvana, as conceived by the Brahmans, may be found in an extract from the Lankavatara, translated by Burnouf, p. 514.

[3] The Vedanta philosophers supposed that after the destruction of ignorance and all its effects, all was again merged into Brahman, the true source of being, thought and happiness.

But while some of the Upanishads, like the Katha, taught the immortality of the soul and the absorption of everything into Brahman, others show that this apparent monotheism is simply pantheism, and that the universe itself is supposed to be Brahma. Not only this, but Brahma is himself represented as dying, as well as the souls which have been absorbed into his substance,

which it repudiated, with a God whom it ignored, therefore the Nirvāṇa of this system could never be interpreted as "absorption into the divine essence." With Buddha, Nirvāṇa must have meant either non-existence or the path that leads to that condition.[1]

"The wise hold that there is really nothing existing, and those whose minds are disgusted with a future existence go out like the lamp. As a flame blown out by the wind goes out, and cannot be considered as existing, even so a Muni, delivered from name and body, cannot be reckoned as existing. Exert thyself, then, being wise; let one having listened to my utterance learn his own extinction."[2]

LITERATURE.

The literature, of course, was largely founded upon these doctrines which existed in some form among the earlier philosophies of India, and the florid description which is often found is also a natural growth of the Indian school of letters.

We have, too, the secret Tāntric doctrines and the elucidation of the ceremonies of Śiva worship, which was the most revolting feature of Brāhmanism.

But we have also portions of books, and in one instance almost a whole Sutta (the Dhamma-pada), treating of morality, virtue, self-control and wisdom. Here is an element which, although a part of the

and in strict accordance with the pantheistic idea the whole universe expires with him, to be reorganized again when he comes from the death state. (See Chandogya Upanishad, 3-14.)

[1] See pp. 126, 132.

[2] Extract from the discourse of Buddha, found in the Sutta-nipata, v. 1069. See also verses 234, 353, 354, 1073, 1061 and many others.

system, is so entirely different from the great mass of Buddhist literature that it cannot be considered as coming from the same source, and it appears to have been derived from a different race. It is a noteworthy fact that we find here many striking similarities to the sentiments of Biblical writers which were given to the world long before the time of Buddha.

ORIGINALITY OF BUDDHA.

It is evident that the principal theories of Buddhism lived in India long before Gautama's time. Atheism and transmigration, the doctrine of karma, the principles of pessimism, the theories of metaphysics, the effort to accumulate merit, and even the idea of Nirvāṇa, were already in existence and ready for his work.

That which was new and original with Buddha was the changing of a philosophical system into a practical doctrine. He took the thoughts of the few and promulgated them among the many. Although he did not wish to abolish caste as a social institution, and though there is no trace of social leveling, or of democratic communism in his discourses, still he opposed the exclusive privileges which were claimed by the Brāhmans and protested against their cruel treatment of the lower castes.

He disregarded the exclusiveness of the priests and addressed himself to all classes, and hence Buddhism was a reaction against Brāhmanism even while retaining much of its faith.

CAUSES OF EXTENSIVE INFLUENCE.

"How a religion," says Max Müller, "which taught the annihilation of all existence, of all thought, of all individuality and personality, as the highest object of all endeavor, could have laid hold of the minds of millions of human beings, and how at the same time, by enforcing the duties of morality, justice, kindness and self-sacrifice, it could have exercised a beneficial influence . . . is a riddle which no one has been able to solve."[1]

Virtue is enjoined, not because it necessarily leads to happiness. On the contrary, happiness is to be shunned, and the only reward of virtue is that it subdues the passions and thus prepares the mind for that knowledge which is to end in complete annihilation or utter extinction. Buddhism says: "Act rightly through your own efforts, and for the final getting rid of all suffering, of all individuality, of all life in yourselves."

Buddha affirmed of himself that he came into the world by the force derived from his own acts. By that force alone he had passed through innumerable bodies of gods, demi-gods, demons, men and animals, until he entered the side of his mother in the form of a white elephant. He declared that all enlightenment and wisdom were to be obtained by his followers through themselves and their own intuitions, and that only after a long and painful discipline in countless successive bodily existences.

[1] F. Max Müller, Chips, Vol. I, p. 243.

He did not admonish his followers to lead a life of usefulness and activity, but to shun the world, to withdraw from it, to become indolent and live as paupers upon the earnings of others.

He did not teach them to expect a world renewed and perfected, but a never-ending succession of evil worlds forever coming into existence, developing, decaying, perishing and reviving, all of them always full of disappointment, illusion, transmutation and everlasting misery.

He did not teach that bodily existence is subject to only one transformation, but he taught the passage through countless bodies of men, animals, demons, ghosts and dwellers in various heavens and hells without any progressive development, but in a constant jumble of metamorphoses. The man who had spent years in one of the heavens was liable to be born the next time as a reptile, or in hell.

He taught that the body, whether of man or of any higher being, can never be the abode of anything but evil; that a man, or even a god, may become an animal of any kind or the most loathsome vermin.

Instead of teaching that all affection should be purified and exalted, he claimed that all affections should be utterly destroyed.

Instead of teaching men to go to work and honorably earn their own bread—instead of admonishing them to provide for their own households, he commanded them to abandon wife and children, and leave them to starvation if need be, while the husband and father begged his own bread from door to door.

Instead of teaching his followers to ask what they should do to inherit eternal life, he taught them to seek for the path to eternal extinction, and proclaimed as the only true creed, the doctrine of the ultimate resolution of everything into nothing, of every entity into pure nonentity.

We may well ask, then, by what means he made his views popular even with the people of India?

It is evident that the system of the Brāhmans had run its course. Their ascendancy had assumed a political character. By means of the laws of caste their influence had pervaded the whole social fabric, not as a healthful influence, but as a deadly poison.

It was impossible for one to assert any freedom of thought or action without being impeded on all sides by the Brāhmanic law, and the oppressed and discontented people were ripe for a change. The ceremonials had become so constant, so expensive and so unendurable, that when Buddha proclaimed them useless the multitudes gladly flocked to his standard.

His success was also greatly accelerated by political events. Chandra-gupta had assumed his supremacy in India in defiance of the laws of caste, which forbade the kingship to any but the military class. Neither he nor his successors could hope for the support of the Brāhmans, therefore his grandson Aśoka gladly availed himself of the influence of the new sect. The low-born king saw his natural allies in the multitude of mendicants who opposed the Brāhmanic law, and would, if possible, set aside the power which denied his right to the throne. He therefore gave all of his influence to the Buddhists, and they soon attained an importance which their founder little anticipated.

It mattered not to the people of India that the expensive gifts with which they had been accustomed to fee the Brāhmans were merely diverted into another channel, and they welcomed the army of beggars who seemed to deliver them from the exactions of the priesthood.

"Those who see in Buddhism not a social but a religious reform have been deceived by the later Buddhist literature, and particularly by the controversies between the Buddhists and Brāhmans, which, in later times, led to the expulsion of the former from India and to the political re-establishment of Brāhmanism."[1]

Buddha began with a very simple creed—only the promulgation of "the four verities." He proclaimed that all existence involved only sorrow and suffering; that sorrow was produced by our affections and desire of any kind, especially the desire for life. He also claimed that our affections must be destroyed in order to destroy the root of sorrow, and that he could teach mankind to eradicate all affection.

This creed was easily understood, and he received people of every caste, who were thus relieved from the expensive and burdensome ceremonies of Brāhmanism. Not only this, but his most enthusiastic devotees were also sure of being supported without work on the charitable contributions of the lay members, and we cannot wonder that the number of his followers rapidly increased, for the doctrine of indolence and inac-

[1] F. Max Müller, Chips, Vol. I, p. 221.

tion is especially attractive to the people of warm climates.

But human nature could not be changed, and the system which began by refusing any form of prayer to the helpless children of earth, soon counted its "praying machines" by thousands. And he who had denied the existence not only of a Creator, but of any absolute being, was himself deified by the hungry hearts of millions who felt the need of a Father to whom they could go with their burdens and their sorrows.

INDEX.

A.

Abhi-dhamma Pitaka, 170.
Achievement, Highest, 31, 39.
Activity, Literary, in the East, 150, n. 153.
Agnosticism, 105, 197.
Ahasuerus, 152, 194.
Alexander, 17.
Alphabet, Indian, 195; Semitic, 194.
Amitabha Buddha, 175; Paradise of, 174.
Amitayur-dhyana, 163, 174, 175.
Amravatti, Relic Mounds in, 48; Buddhist Carvings at, 86.
Ananda, 51, 79, 96, 145, 147, 164.
Ancient Empires, n. 192, n. 193.
Anguttara Nikaya, 86, 163.
Animals, Sacred, 81, 103; veneration for, 102.
Anomadassin, 36.
Antelope, the Wily, 82, 93.
Arahats, 59, 130, 131.
Artaxerxes Longimanus, n. 195.
Asankheyyas, 32.
Asankheyya Sutta, n. 85.
Arabian Nights, n. 99.
Asceticism, 63, 68, 69.
Asia, Eastern, 14, 18.
Asiatic Society of Bengal, 24; Journal of, n. 56; of London, 24.
Asoka, 17, 172, 207.
Asuras, 111.
Assyrians, 194.
Assyrian Tablets, n. 153.
Atheism, 19, 104, 107, 108, 109, 198, n. 204.
Attavada, 75.
Austerities, 20, 69.
Avalokitesvara, eleven heads of, 113.

B.

Babylonia, 192.
Babylonians, 194.
Baskets, Three, 155, 195.
Bas-reliefs Illustrating Birth Stories, 86.
Bats, Five Hundred, 160.
Belief, Orthodox, 87.
Benares, 65, 97; Discourse at, 71 73.
Bhagavad-gita, n. 70.
Bharhut, Buddhist carvings at, 86, n. 92, 103; Great Tope at, n 101.
Bigandet, 25.
Births, Series of, 32, 87, 88, 103.
Birth Stories, 33, 82, 101.
Bodhisat, 35, 46, 50, 52, 53, 56: Shrewdness of, 90, 94, 96, 98, 101.
Bo-tree, 55, 57, 70, 113.
Book of the Great Decease, 43, 77, 163, 164.
Bowls, care of, 150, 156.
Borrower, Universal, 196.
Brahma, Archangel, 47, 56, n. 70, 71, 77, 79, 109; gods, 89, 109, 110.
Brahmans, 16, 18, 69, 83, 89, 108, 151, 199, 204, 207.
Brahmanism, 14, 18, 28, 69, 83, 118, 120, 126, 191, 201, 202, 208; Austerities of, 69; Indebtedness to, 151, 183.

Brahma-jala Sutta, n. 85, 154.
British Museum, 113.
Brothers, Lay, 134.
Buddha Gautama, Asceticism of, 63, 68; Atheism of, 19, 108; Birth of, 42, 46, 47, 63, 64, 66; Numerous dates assigned to birth of, 64, n. 80; Biography of, 43, 63, 81; Benevolence of, 35, 40, 47, 57, 202; Buddhistic Account of, 42; Former Births of, 46, n. 61, 81, 82, 84, 89, 101; Five Human, 110; Death of, 43, 63, 80; Historic Sketch of, 63; Originality of, 198, 204; Images of, 112; Indebtedness to Brahmanism, 151, 183.
Buddha-karita, 46, n. 49, n. 53, 121, 163, 172.
Buddha Names, Allegorical, 65.
Buddhas, Future, 32; Numerous, 31, 38, 40.
Buddha, Physical Signs of, 42, 48, 59, 173, 176; Predecessors of, 31, 38, 174; Prophecy of, 147; Teachings of, 60, 71, 73, 75, 77, 101, 107, 122, 124, 125, 127, 135, 136, 139, 142, 146, 156, 158, 162, 164, 167, 169.
Buddhas, Three, 37, 38; Wonders of, 150, 159.
Buddha-ghosha, 155, 171.
Buddha-vansa, 168.
Buddhism, A Blessing to India, 13, 18, 20, 30; A Benefit to Women, 13, 21; Critical Study of, 13, 23; In China, 17, 30; Disappearance from India, 28; Highest Achievement of, 39, 40, 41; Nihilism of, 129, 205; Number of Adherents, 7, 13, 27; Origin and Teachings, 13, 31, 42, 82, 104, 133, 156, 163; Primitive, 13, 15, 20, 168, 198; Summum bonum of, 20, 130, 132.
Buddhists, Canon of, 8, 38, 45; Canon Perpetuated Orally, 42, 88, 161.
Buddhist Literature, 25, 27, 43, 44, 77, 87, 104, 137, 150, 163, 183.
Buddhist Scriptures, Extent of, 153.
Buddhists, Northern, 44, 115, 132; Southern, 50.
Bull who won the Bet, 82, 94.
Burmah, 15, 29.
Burmese, 27.
Burnouf, 9, 26, n. 35, 50, 130, 132, 182.

C.

Calcutta, 24.
Canon, Date of, 150, 154; Perpetuated Orally, 17, 42, 43, 88, 152, 161.
Caste, 16, 17, 18, 85, 204, 207.
Catholicism, 15.
Causes of Extensive Influence, 198, 205.
Ceylon, 15, 18, 25, 28, 64, 110.
Chandra-gupta, 17.
Channa, 53, 54, 207.
Chicago Public Library, 8.
China, 14, 24, 28, 150, 174; Buddhism a disturbing influence in, 30.
Childers, 25, 128, 131.
Christ, 190.
Christianity, 28, 29, n. 67, 197.
Chiliocosm, 39.
Commandments, Ten, 125, 189.
Confession, 137, 138, 146.
Confucius, 30, 150, 190.
Confucianism, 29, 201.
Congress of Religions, 105.
Converts, First, 154.
Contrasts, Striking, 181.
Councils, 17, 45, 86, 87, 154.
Cowell, Prof. E. B., 25, n. 100.
Clothing, Unsanitary, 141, 142.

D.

Daniel, 150, 194.
Darius, 150, 194.
Dates, Numerous, 64, n. 80.
Davids, T. W. Rhys, 25, 33, 44,

45, 46, 87, 101, 130, 152, 153, 191, 193.
Delusion, 106, 107.
Demon, Sharp-fanged, 35; Worship, 15, 110, 112, 197.
Demerit, 125, 201, 202.
Deva-datta, 92, 93; Punishment of, 121.
Deva-loka, 38.
Dhamma-pada, n. 71, 110, 120, 154, 163, 167, 181, 182, 185, 188, 190, 196, 203.
Dhammas, Nine, 44.
Diacritical Points, 11.
Diamond-cutter, 104, 180.
Dipavamsa, n. 48, 85.
Dipankara, 31, 32, 34, 59.
Discourse at Benares, 63, 71.
Dukkata, 156 158.

E.

Earthquakes, Cause of, 163, 164.
East India Company, 24.
Ecclesiastes, n. 190.
Egypt, 82, n. 153, 185.
Egyptians, 82, 83, 200.
Eitel's Lectures, n. 102.
Elephant, White, 47, 86, 172, 205.
Enlightenment, 16, 63, 70, n. 122, 166, 205.
Escape, the, 42, 53.
Ethics, Code of, 125, 151.
Ethiopia, 152, 194.
Evidences, Chronological, 155.
Eye of Truth, 136.
Exodus, n. 189.

F.

Fa Hian, n. 64, 152.
Fatal Meal, 77.
Fausböll, 25.
Fairy, or devata, 165.
Fire Sermon, 62, 75.
First Path, fruit of, 60.
First Writings, date of 43.
Fish, Lament of, 97; and his Wife, 82, 96.
Flesh, of dogs, 140; human, 141; of lions, 140; of serpents, 140.
Foucaux, 45
Four Truths, 76.
Freer, n. 45.
Frog born into one of the heavens, 161.
Fundamental Prohibitions, 125.

G.

Gautama, 8, 31, 32, 33, 36, 37, 38, 42, 51, 55, 66, 67, 68, 70, 86, 89, 93, 184, 191, 199, 200, 204.
Gautami, 145, 146.
Gemera, n. 195.
Godoshiu Sect, 174.
Gogerly, 25.
Gopa, 50.
Gordon, Surgeon-General, 191, 192.
Gospels, Similarities to, 67.
Greece, 150, 192.
Greeks, 28.

H.

Heaven, 104, 118, 119.
Hebrews, 150, 189.
Hell, 114, 120.
Hells, thirty-six, 121; of Brahmanism, 121; Buddha's description of, 122.
Herodotus, 82.
Hinduism, 14, 29, 118, 201.
Hindustan, 16.
Hindu gods recognized by Buddha, 108, 118.
Hodgson, 154.
Historic Sense, 42.

I.

Idolatry, 104, 112.
Idols, 113, 115, 199.
Incantations, 23.
Indian Antiquary, n. 100.
India, 3, 13, 14, 17, 18, 23, 30, 42, 88, 90, 102, 110, 112, 129, 142, 150, 152, 192, 194, 195, 207.
Indra, 54, 185.

Infants, Sacrifice of, 23.
Influence of Christian and Mohammedan Thought, 109.
Institute, Victoria, 9.
Integrity of the Texts, 161.
International Congress of Orientalists, n. 29, n. 30, n. 39, n. 40.
Introduction à l'Histoire du Buddhism, 25.
Isaiah, 186.

J.

Jainism, 29.
Japan, 14, 15, 24, 29.
Jatakas, 33, 42, 45, 46, 82, 85, 163, 164, 168, 191; early collections of, 86.
Jetavana, 93, 96, 100.
Jews, the, 15, 191, 193, 194.
Josephus, 193.
Judge, the Wise, 99.
Julien, Stanislaus, 27.

K.

Kalpa, n. 31, 32.
Kapila, doctrines of, 65.
Kanishka, King, 45, 171, 172.
Kanjur, 154.
Kanthaka, 53, 54.
Karma, 84, 107, 120, 175, 200, 204.
Kassapa, 59, 159, 160.
Kashmir, King of, 171.
Kern, 25, 64.
Khandhaka, 156.
Khuddaka-patha, 163.
Kings, Book of, 98, 191.
Koeppen, n. 114.
Konagamana, 62.
Kondanna, 31, 34, 72.
Kasola, 66.
Kulla-vagga, 156, n. 157, n. 158.
Kunda, 78.

L.

Lalita Vistara, 42, 44, 46, n. 48, n. 49, n. 51, 55, n. 85, 174.
Lamas, 115.
Lama, Grand, 15.
Lassen, 25, 193.
Language, Mongolian, 25.
Lawgiver, Jewish, 125.
Laws, Unsanitary, 138.
Legge, Dr. James, 9, 28, 30, n. 38, n. 39, n. 40, n. 67, n. 111.
Leviticus, n. 189. n. 190.
Liberty, Social, 20.
Literature, Buddhist, 150, 168, 196, 198, 203; Tantra, 149, 163, 181, 182, 196; Semitic, 98.
Literary Record, Trübner's, n. 129.

M.

Magic, 110.
Maha-yana, 106, 110, 163, 171.
Mahendra, 171.
Maha-vagga, 43, n. 53, n. 58, 71, 75, 122, 139, 156, 175.
Maha-parinibbana-Suttana, 77, n. 79, 163, 164, n. 166.
Mahavamsa, n. 43.
Mahoragas, 111.
Maitreya, 112.
Majjhima, 163.
Mara, 55, 57, 79, 108, 110, 127.
Mango grove, 78.
Mangala, 31, 34, 35.
Manuscript, Indian, 167.
Manifestations, Sphere of, 31, 38.
Matthew, 190.
Marriages, Child, 22.
Maya, 66, 67.
Meal, the Fatal, 63, 65, 77.
Medians, 194.
Medical Knowledge of Ancient India, 191.
Medicines, Loathsome, 141.
Megillah, n. 195.
Mendicants, Order of, 61, 79.
Memories of Pre-existent Conditions, 85.
Metaphysics, 102, 104, 108, 122, 177, 184, 198, 200.
Metaphysician, Buddhist, 129.
Merit, Accumulation of, 22, 198, 201, 202.
Meru Mountain, 119.

Mesopotamia, n. 153, 193.
Mishna, n. 195.
Mitford, 150.
Mohammedanism, 28.
Monastery, First, 42, 61.
Mongolia, 30
Monks, Directions for, 133, 137; Frauds Perpetrated by, 112; Ordination of, 133, 134; Order of, 114, 148; Protection of, from Serpents, 133; Unsanitary Clothing of, 133; Unsanitary Laws for, 133.
Monkhood, 21, 133; Formula for Admission, 77, 134; Results of, 133, 148.
Monkeys and the Demon, 82, 90.
Morality, 104, 125, 182.
Morris, 25.
Moses, 191, 189.
Mucalinda, the Snake King, 58, 111; Tree, 58.
Mugheir, 192.
Müller, Prof. F. Max, 9, 11, 25, 27, 63, 104, 129, 132, 151, 155, 175, 177, 183, 193.
Myth, Theory of, 63.

N.

Naga, 35, 159; Worship, 15, 111.
Naga-kanyas, or female Nagas, 111.
Nanda, King, 16.
Nandi Visala, 95, 96.
Nanjio, Bunyiu, n. 38, n. 175.
Narada, 36.
Nepal, 24, 44, 110, 154.
Nepalese Sanskrit Works, 171.
Nikanyas, 154.
Nirvana, 39, 40, 41, 42, 103, 104, 124, 126, 131, 181, 185, 198, 201, 202, 204; Contradictory Teaching of Buddhistic Authorities, 127, 128; Not Original with Buddha, 126; Various Theories Concerning, 127, 128; Signification of, 126.
Non-existence of the Soul, 63, 74, 106.
Nuns, 21, 133; Indebted to Ananda, 145; Rules pertaining to, 146.
Northern School, 163.

O.

Occult Meaning, n. 114.
Offense, Dukkata, 136.
Oldenberg, Dr., 9, 25, 43, 55, 65, 68, 70, 90, 124, 125, 128, 152.
Om! mani padme Hum! 114, 115.
Ophir, 193.
Order, Growth of, 134.
Origin and Growth of Religion, n. 44, n. 84.
Orthodox Belief, 82.
Oxford University, 28.

P.

Padmuttara, 31, 36.
Paduma, 36.
Pali, 25, 27; Canon, 25, 150, 154, 155; Characters, 25; Early Texts, 42, 43, 55, 67, 70, 155, 159, 160, 161, 163, 168, 167, 169; Pitakas, 68, 84, 86, 88; Suttas, 101.
Palestine, n. 153, 192, 194.
Path, Eight-fold, 71, 125, 182.
Patimakkha, 137, 164.
Pathoma Sompothiyan, n, 47.
Parimitas, 126.
Pari-nirvana, 103, 104, 131.
Parivara-patha, 156.
Parajika Books, 149, 182.
Patna, Council of, 87.
Pattini, goddess, 110.
Philosophies, 7, 184, 191.
Phœnicia, 192.
Phœnicians, 192.
Persians, 28, 194.
Pessimism, 104, 117, 118, 184, 197, 198, 206, 208.
Perfections, Ten, 92.
Pitaka, Second, 163; Third, 163, 170; Vinaya, 94, 108, 150, 155.

Pippala, or Pipal Tree, 69, 113.
Pisacas, 111.
Possible Borrowing from Semitic Literature, 98.
Possible Sources of Information, 182, 192.
Polytheism, 104, 109, 118, 119, 197.
Prayer, 104, 114, 116, 209; Bells, 116; Jewel, 114; Wheels, 30, 115, 209.
Pragna-paramita, 163, 180.
Pretas, 111.
Priesthood, Brahmanic, 17, 18, 20.
Pronunciation, 11.
Prophecy of Buddha, 133, 147.
Proverbs, 186, 187, 188, n. 189, 190.
Psalms, n. 187, n. 188, n. 189, n. 190.
Psalmist, 187, 188, 189.
Pujawaliya, n, 49.
Punishment, 120, 122, 123, 163, 167, 168
Pyrrhonism, Metaphysical, 129.

R.

Races, Semitic, 153.
Rahula, 51, 60, 61, 68.
Ragnun, Great Bell at, 37.
Rajendra-lala Mitra, 44.
Rajayatana Tree, 58.
Rakshasas, 111.
Recitation of the Law, 15, 16, 160.
Refuge in Buddha, 77; in Law, 77; in Order, 77.
Regions of Desire, 39; of Form, 39; Without Form, 39.
Relic Mounds, 47,
Republicanism, Doctrines of, 16.
Renan, 22, 116.
Renunciation, Great, 42, 52.
Return Home, 42, 59.
Resources, Four, 135, 136.
Revata, 31, 36.
Rig-veda, 83.
Ritter, Carl Von, 193.
Rites and Ceremonies, 75.
Ritual, Vedic, 16.
Robes, Directions for Making, 138.
Roman, 28.
Rome, Church of, 15.
Rugs, Directions for Making, 37.

S.

Sabbasava Sutta, 106.
Saddharma Pundarika, 86.
Sacred Books of the East, 8, n. 43, n. 46, n. 85, n. 165, n. 109, n. 165.
Sacrifices, 110.
Saint Hilaire, Barthélemy, 9, 29, n. 67, 130.
Saivism, 110, 117, 197.
Sakka, King of the Devas, 159, 160.
Saktism, 110, 197.
Sakwala, 56.
Sakya-muni, 29, 64, 65.
Sakya-sina, 64.
Sakyas, 50, 64, 66.
Salvation, 104, 124.
Samana-phala-sutta, n. 84, 154.
Samyutta Nikaya, n. 128.
Sanchi, 48, 86.
Sankhya, n. 114, 183, 197, 199.
Sara-sagraha, n. 43.
Satapatha-brahmana, 183.
Sayce, Prof. A. H., 9, n. 153, 192, 193.
Scholars, Oriental, 10, 24, 87.
Schilling, Baron, 115.
Schools of Thought, 17.
Science of Religion, n. 43.
Schlagintweit, Dr., n. 115.
Schmidt, 24.
Scriptures, Buddhist, 17, 42, 43, 86, 150, 154, 161; Extent of, 150.
Senart, 28, n. 45, 64.
Serpents, Five Kinds of, 146; Four Royal Breeds of, 143; How they may obtain Human Nature, 144; Protection from,

142, 143; Who joined the Order, 133, 143.
Sex, Change of, 22, 198.
Shamanism, 15.
Shintoism, 15.
Siam, 15.
Siddhata, 37.
Similarities to the Gospels, 67; to Old Testament Teaching, 183, 186, 204.
Sikhin, 61.
Singhalese, 27.
Siva, 14, 15, 110, 182, 196, 203.
Skandhas, 39, 74, n. 180.
Sobhita, 31, 36.
Societé Asiatique, 24, 25.
Socrates, 150.
Solomon, 186, 188, 191, 192.
Solomon, Judgment of, 98.
Soul, Heresy of Belief in, 74; Non-existence of, 63, 74, 106, 200.
Souphir, 193.
Studies in Religious History, n. 22, n. 117.
Subha-sutta, 154.
Sudra, 16, 17.
Suddhodana, 66, 172.
Sujata, 31, 37.
Sukhavati-vyhua, 32, 174.
Sumana, 31, 35, 36.
Summary, 183, 195.
Sumedha, 31, 36.
Sumeru Mountain, 37.
Sutta, Nipata, 154, 163, 164, 168; Extracts from, 169; Pitaka, n. 74.
Suttee, Prevalence of, 23, 199.
Sutras, Discourses of Buddha, 155.
Sutra Period, 151.
Sravasti, 37.

T.

Tabernacle, 191.
Talmud, n. 195.
Tanjur, 154.
Tantra Literature, 149, 163, 182.
Tantric Doctrines, 203.
Tantrism, 110, 148.
Taoist, 14.
Taoism, 28.
Tathagata, 40, 43, 108, 147; Final Extinction of, 77, 79, 127.
Tel-el-Amarna, n. 153.
Temple, Hindu, 191.
Temptation, Great, 42, 55, 173.
Text, Integrity of, 150.
Texts, Vinaya, 94, 108, 150, 155, 161.
Tibet, 15, 20.
Tibetans, 154; Canon of, 24.
Tooth Sticks, 150, 158.
Tradition, Vedic, 48.
Transmigration, 23, 26, 70, 82, 84, 198, 200, 201, 204, 205, 206; Origin of the Theory, 82; Relief from, 63, 71, 76, 118.
Tri-pitaka, 150, 155, 171, 181, 182.
Truths, Four, 71, 76.

U.

Upanishads, 83, 150, 200.
Upasampada, 136, 137, 144.
Universal Spirit, 202.
Unsanitary Clothing, 133, 142; Food, 139, 140; Laws, 133, 136.

V.

Vagrakkhedika, 104, 163, 177; Doctrinal Teaching of, 163, 178.
Various Forms Assumed, 82, 88.
Vedas, 150, 199.
Vedic Hymns, 151; Philosophy, 199; Sacrifices, 199.
Vessabhu, 62.
Vesali, Council of, 86, 88.
Victoria Institute, 9, 191, 192.
Vibhanga, 156.
Vinaya Pitaka, 94, 108, 162, 196.
Vishnu, 14.
Vispassin, 37, 61.
Visions, Four, 42, 52, 68.

W.

Was, the Rainy Season, 100.
Weber, 25.
Williams, Sir Monier Monier-, 9, 11, 25, n. 31, 43, 44, 45, 89, 131, 149, 152, 197.
Wilson, Prof. H. H., 44.
Wise Judge, 82.
Wisdom, Supreme, 32.
Woman, Benefit to, 3, 13, 21, 198.
Writing, Art of, 151.

X.

Xerxes, 152, 194.

Y.

Yakshas, n. 99.
Yakshini, 99, 100.
Yama, 120.
Yasodhara, 50, 51; Lament of, 54, 173.
Yoga, 20.

Z.

Zoroaster, 150.
Zoroastrianism, 28, 201.